'In 2024, Lee Gatiss addressed an assembled gathering of all the pastors and leaders of the Anglican Province of Chile. He delighted us and changed our lives with a fresh appreciation of Cranmer's Thirty-nine Articles and basic Anglican Christology. He managed this cross-cultural task, with his very direct style of cheerful communication that "digs deep" (a phrase he uses often) into Scripture's secrets behind its plain teachings, widely referencing serious figures in church history and literature. He does a similar job with this latest book, *Living to Please God*, where he explores the novel question of how we can possibly please an already infinitely happy God. His digging takes us beyond the obvious self-centred understanding of happiness prevalent today (even in churches) and is summed up in his personal rendering of the Westminster Catechism's opening statement: "The chief end of man is to know God and be enjoyed by him forever." Be it in family, sexual relationships, or money matters, he argues that only those "in Christ", the Son who pleased the Father in every way, can we also please God. Again, the story of the violinist changed my life! Taste and see!'

Alfredo Cooper, Auxiliary Bishop of Santiago, Chile

'Hopefully every Christian wants to please God, but often we need help to know what this looks like in practice. Biblically faithful, helpfully fresh and contemporary (while engaging with the past), *Living to Please God* paints a beautiful picture of the God-pleasing life and encourages us to seek the grace to live more truly for God's pleasure.'

Donald John MacLean, President, Westminster Seminary, UK

LIVING TO PLEASE GOD

Life for a higher purpose
and pleasure

Lee Gatiss

INTER-VARSITY PRESS
SPCK Group, Studio 101, The Record Hall, 16–16A Baldwin's Gardens, London
EC1N 7RJ, England
Email: ivp@ivpbooks.com
Website: www.ivpbooks.com

First published 2025

British Library Cataloguing-in-Publication Data
A catalogue record for this book is available from the British Library.

ISBN: 978-1-78974-539-9
eBook ISBN: 978-1-78974-540-5

Set in 10.25/13.75 Minion Pro
Typeset in Great Britain by Fakenham Prepress Solutions, Fakenham
Printed in Great Britain by Clays Ltd, Bungay, Suffolk

Produced on paper from sustainable sources

*Inter-Varsity Press publishes Christian books that are true to the Bible and that
communicate the gospel, develop discipleship and strengthen the church for its mission in
the world.*

*IVP originated within the Inter-Varsity Fellowship, now the Universities and Colleges
Christian Fellowship, a student movement connecting Christian Unions in universities
and colleges throughout Great Britain, and a member movement of the International
Fellowship of Evangelical Students. Website: www.uccf.org.uk. That historic association
is maintained, and all senior IVP staff and committee members subscribe to the UCCF
Basis of Faith*

Contents

Dedication

For the wonderful men and women it's been my pleasure to serve with on the staff of Church Society over the last 12 years: Claire Alldritt, Sophie Barker, Kirsty Birkett, Tony Cannon, Ros Clarke, Marcus Cobb, George Crowder, Mike Locke, Marion Mason, David Meager, Chris Moore, Jemima Sohn, and Mark Wallace. Thank you for your hard work and dedication to the task of reforming and renewing the Church of England in biblical faith.

1

God's happiness

I have no need of a bull from your stall
  or of goats from your pens,
for every animal of the forest is mine,
  and the cattle on a thousand hills.
I know every bird in the mountains,
  and the insects in the fields are mine.
If I were hungry I would not tell you,
  for the world is mine, and all that is in it.
Do I eat the flesh of bulls
  or drink the blood of goats?

Sacrifice thank offerings to God,
  fulfill your vows to the Most High,
and call on me in the day of trouble;
  I will deliver you, and you will honor me.
(Psalm 50:9–15)

If God followed you on social media, what would he make of your posts? What would he like and what would he frown at? Would he repost or share your contributions, or make some kind of comment on them along with everyone else?

Sometimes social media informs me that one (or twenty-three) of my friends have liked a certain product or started following a particular account. The implication is clear: would I care to do the same? What if it notified me of the things which God had liked today or commented on at some point? What would I do with that kind of data?

I'm not trying to scare you into conducting a godliness audit of your social media interaction! Though that's not necessarily a bad idea.[1] Rather, I want to get us thinking about the more basic question: does God like or dislike the things we say, or think, or do? And if so, how can we tell? Short of him actually opening up an account on Facebook or Instagram, is there a way to know how he views things? Or are we left to guess and speculate using our own ideas and imaginations: 'I *think* God will like this,' or '*I'm* not sure he'd like that very much'?

The answer, of course, is to be found primarily in 'God-breathed' Scripture (2 Timothy 3:16). As the Reformer Martin Luther (1483– 1546) rightly said, 'It is not man's business to determine what pleases God; it is the business of God alone.'[2] As we will discover, there are several different ways in which God's word speaks of his approval of something. God says someone 'finds favour' with him, or that something gives him pleasure, he delights in it, or he is happy. The Bible talks about how something is good in God's eyes, or acceptable, or pleasing to him. We have thumbs-up and laughing reactions on Facebook and other social media to express our feelings, but God uses a number of different words and phrases to express his likes and his dislikes – not just a crying emoji or an angry face. He is simultaneously both much more subtle and demonstrably clear.

Studying words

In days gone by, the idea of studying particular words in the Bible was very popular. Many sermons and books were just word studies, like extended dictionary articles with applications tagged

---

1 I found Tony Reinke's *12 Ways Your Phone Is Changing You* (Wheaton, IL: Crossway, 2017) a helpful place to start thinking about better smartphone habits.

2 Martin Luther, *Luther's Works*, ed. J. J. Pelikan, H. C. Oswald and H. T. Lehmann (St Louis, MO: Concordia, 1999), 16:35 (in his lecture on Isaiah 2:8).

on. That's not my intention in this book. There were certain dangers associated with that approach to the Bible which have led to its being abandoned in many parts of the Church. Often a word would be defined without paying attention to the context in which it was used. Or it was just assumed a word meant the same thing in one place as it did in another, when that was not necessarily the case. Bible words were given dictionary meanings, that is, the meanings they had in the English of the day, rather than the meanings they have in the Bible itself.

There are other errors and difficulties associated with word studies. But we mustn't be so cautious of the potential mistakes we could make that we altogether neglect studying God's actual words. Otherwise, we would never open the Bible and start reading for fear of making a mistake. 'Every word of God is flawless', says Proverbs 30:5, so we can deeply ponder every last one and chew on all of them in their splendidly rich variety, and they will not ultimately lead us astray.

What we are going to do in this book is unpack the whole concept or theme of living to please God, not just one particular word as it turns up in random places throughout the Bible. Naturally, we will try to pay attention to the context as much as possible too, within the constraints of a short book. So this is not what is sometimes called systematic theology as such. It's more 'biblical theology'. That is, we're trying to discover the theology of pleasing God as it is presented by the Bible books themselves, paying due attention to their contexts and their place in the history of God's plan.

Part of this must be to acknowledge that there is a shift of some kind from Old Testament to New. There is a progression in the Bible's revelation of God, so that we know more about what pleases him at the end than we do at the beginning. Plus, we have Jesus in the middle, so to speak, who shows us the way more perfectly, and sends his Spirit to help us. These are all vitally important things to take note of when we're trying to work out what makes

3

God happy. We can't necessarily just lift things straight out of the Old Testament and apply them directly to us today without thinking about whether something significant has changed in the meantime.

So we might come across a passage in the Old Testament which says God is pleased when people sacrifice bulls and goats and sheep, or when they keep the Sabbath. We can't just lift those texts straight out of the Old Testament and say God is still pleased with animal sacrifices and keeping Saturday special. The meaning of both sacrifices and special days today has to take account of the radical change to the whole Old Testament system brought about by Jesus. After all, God's people used not to be allowed to eat shellfish or pork (see the dietary laws in the book of Leviticus); but Jesus 'declared all foods clean' for us (Mark 7:19). Yet in both Old and New Testaments, certain things also remain the same: Jesus did not declare all sexual practices clean, for example, or do away with the commandment against theft.

I should also say at this point that ever since I started thinking seriously about this biblical theme, I have become sensitive to it in all my reading. So as I've dug into the great theological and devotional literature over the last two decades and more, I have spotted it coming up time and time again. I hope to share with you some of the best reflections on this topic from older Christian writers too, whom I have found very helpful in the development of my own thinking and Christian living. After all, our generation is not the first to ever read and reflect on God's word, and as it says in Job 8:8–9: 'Ask the former generation and find out what their ancestors learned, for we were born only yesterday and know nothing, and our days on earth are but a shadow.' There is humility and wisdom in hearing what others have found on this topic, as on many others. Not because they have more authority than God's word (as if!), but because they studied it and tried to live it, just as we do. It also demonstrates very clearly that I'm definitely not the first to see how important this theme of living to please God is in the Bible.[3]

God's emotional language

Thinking about pleasing God a bit further, however, leads to some tricky questions about divine emotions and divine language. We need to look at these briefly, before we dig in to the Bible's teaching on this subject in more detail, because we don't want to draw false conclusions from what we find.

We chase after certain things because we think they will make us happy: knowledge, power, wealth, respect, celebrity, relationships – these things fuel our ambitions and give us pleasure. But does God need any of these things? He knows everything. He governs the whole universe. He's completely self-sufficient, and doesn't need us or anything else to 'complete' him (see Psalm 50, for example, which we'll come back to later). He is at peace with himself and utterly content, 'the essence of happiness' as one early Christian writer called Boethius (480–524) put it.[4] The great medieval theologian Thomas Aquinas (1225–1274) said anything that could possibly make one happy (delight, riches, power, dignity, fame) pre-exists wholly and in a more eminent degree in God.[5] He is utterly blessed and self-sufficient (Acts 17:24–5; Romans 11:36; 1 Timothy 6:15).

So when Scripture talks about us displeasing God, it's not as if what we do can really harm God and drag him down. He is not anxiously hanging on our every word, desperately waiting for us

---

3 I'm including footnotes here so you can find where any quotations have come from. But if footnotes scare you, just ignore them and trust me!

4 See Boethius, *The Consolation of Philosophy*, ed. and tr. V. E. Watts (London: Penguin, 1999), pp. 100–1 (3.10). This chapter owes a great deal to my article 'Pleasing the Impassible God' in *Foundations* 79 (Autumn 2020), pp. 3–13.

5 See this idea of God's perfect 'beatitude' or happiness, contrasted with ours, in Thomas Aquinas, *Summa Theologiae*, 1a.26.4.

to make him happy to prevent him from feeling sad, lonely and incomplete. As Job 35:6–8 says:

> If you sin, how does that affect him?
>> If your sins are many, what does that do to him?
> If you are righteous, what do you give to him,
>> or what does he receive from your hand?
> Your wickedness only affects humans like yourself,
>> and your righteousness only other people.

When the Bible says something we do pleases God, it is not saying God changes his facial expression from a frowny face to a smiley one every time he assesses our thoughts, words and deeds. He is not clicking a series of thumbs-up or thumbs-down emojis to express his constantly changing feelings about your actions every second of the day. This is metaphorical language. It is communication designed to convey something to us mere mortals that is real, but utterly sublime. He speaks in a way we can grasp, accommodated to our human understanding.

As he communicates to us in this clear and beautiful way, God is not revealing absolutely everything about his inner being. We couldn't take all that. But he is telling us something true, in such a way that our mortal capacity can handle it. As the early church theologian Dionysius put it, 'We cannot be enlightened by the divine rays except they be hidden within the covering of many sacred veils.'[6] This is why Scripture expounds spiritual truths using figures of speech, including the somewhat paradoxical idea of pleasing the already infinitely happy God. It takes something we are familiar with from our everyday relational life and uses it to convey something about God that is useful

---

6 See Dionysius the Areopagite, *On the Heavenly Hierarchy*, 1.2, as cited in Thomas Aquinas, *Summa Theologiae Prima Pars, 1–49*, ed. John Mortensen and Enrique Alarcón, tr. Laurence Shapcote; Latin/English Edition of the Works of St. Thomas Aquinas, vol. 13 (Lander, WY: Aquinas Institute, 2012), p. 13 (1a.1.9).

and joyful for us to know. God's word tailors its language to our capacity to understand, and is phrased for our spiritual advantage. When he speaks to us, it is not in full-blown, raw and concentrated majesty, because we could hardly bear that (see Exodus 20:18–19). Instead, he considers our finite human capacity and the benefits he wishes to convey to us, and communicates appropriately.[7] As the Reformation writer John Calvin (1509–64) puts this:

> For who even of slight intelligence does not understand that, as nurses commonly do with infants, God is wont [accustomed] in a measure to 'lisp' in speaking to us? Thus such forms of speaking do not so much express clearly what God is like as accommodate the knowledge of him to our slight capacity. To do this he must descend far beneath his loftiness.[8]

Technically, this idea of God expressing his 'feelings' in human clothing is called anthropopathism. That is, ascribing human emotions to God, just as anthropomorphism is ascribing human shape to God. (Don't you love these big words?!) We know from the Bible as a whole that God is spirit (John 4:24), and so does not literally have hands, eyes or ears (or feathers and wings) despite the Bible speaking of us being in the shadow of his wings (Psalm 36:7; 91:4) or of him rolling up his sleeves to bare his holy arm (Psalm 98:1; Isaiah 52:10). So in the same way, we must be careful not to press the language of divine emotion or pleasure too much or too far beyond its biblical purpose. Otherwise, we may end up with a misshapen understanding of God's inner self.

So we mustn't reduce God's ineffable being to our very effable and fallible level. His emotional life is infinitely rich and far more

---

7 See the early Christian thinker Origen, *Against Celsus*, 4.71–2 on this idea, in *The Ante-Nicene Fathers*, vol. 4, ed. A. Roberts, J. Donaldson and A. C. Coxe, tr. F. Crombie (Buffalo, NY: Christian Literature Company, 1885), 4:529–30.

8 John Calvin, *Institutes of the Christian Religion*, ed. J. T. McNeill, tr. F. L. Battles (Louisville, KY: Westminster John Knox Press, 2011), 1:121 (1.13.1).

complex than ours in a way we can only begin to comprehend. Deep study of God's self-revelation in Scripture is the best way for us to make a start on this, but believers will still be meditating on it in glory for thousands and thousands of years. He is an inexhaustible fountain of wonder and goodness.

God's moods

As all parents know, bringing up children can be a tiring and frustrating business. It often leaves us exhausted and moody. When I'm rested and calm, I can be cheerful and generous to my kids; later in the day, when they've been arguing or eating all the food in my fridge, maybe not so much. But God is not like me. In himself, he does not change (Malachi 3:6, James 1:17). He is not vulnerable to bouts of unhappiness, despair or depression because we have been naughty, cruel or unfaithful. Rather, when his word says that we please God, or that he delights in us, the idea is that our actions resonate with the harmony of God himself. Or that he will react in a *similar* way to how we react when we feel such emotions as pleasure or disgust. As the renowned Anglican preacher Charles Simeon (1759–1836) put it, 'When we speak of any thing being "an abomination" or "a delight" to God, we mean only, that he will act in reference to that thing as we should towards any thing which excited such feelings in our minds.'[9]

So, for example, when we are told not to grieve the Holy Spirit by our bitter interactions with one another (Ephesians 4:30), this is metaphorical language designed to teach us something. It means the Spirit's reaction to that unkind behaviour is akin to our human emotion of grief. When I am saddened or angered by the words of people on social media, I can unfollow or unfriend them, or even block them altogether. So, as Aquinas says, this text does not mean

9 Charles Simeon, *Horae Homileticae: Proverbs to Isaiah XXVI* (London: Holdsworth & Ball, 1833), p. 154.

God is susceptible to outbursts of passion in reaction to our sins: 'When some person is saddened he withdraws from whoever is depressing him. Likewise does the Holy Spirit withdraw from one who is sinning … Thus the meaning of "do not grieve the Holy Spirit" is: do not chase him away or reject him through sin.'[10] So it's not about protecting God the Holy Spirit's fragile mood. In some way it is about doing what is best for ourselves, because grieving him will not be good for us.

On the other hand, in the person of his Son, God literally does have human form and human emotions. In his earthly ministry, Jesus was perfectly capable of expressing his displeasure. It was clear what pleased, angered or upset him. In him we can see something of God's emotional life literally incarnate: made flesh. Again, the idea is that if he is pleased with you, that's good for you; if he's not, it would be better for you if you changed your ways. So in the Gospels, Jesus isn't simply showing us that he's a touchy-feely guy in tune with his inner feelings. Jesus' emotions teach us something about what we should care about or watch out for too.

So these are some of the things we need to be aware of and keep in the back of our minds as we explore what the Bible says about pleasing God. We need to remember the nature of God (who he is), as well as the nature of his word to us (its trustworthy and clear but 'lisping' quality). These theological truths will keep us anchored as we begin to unwrap the various colourful and powerful ways that Scripture preaches to us on this subject.

Prayer

Almighty and eternal Father,
who does not change like shifting shadows or the tides of the sea:
give us grace

---

10 Thomas Aquinas, *Commentary on the Letters of Saint Paul to the Galatians and Ephesians*, tr. F. R. Larcher and M. L. Lamb (Lander, WY: Aquinas Institute, 2012), p. 298.

so to understand your clear and unerring word
that we may know you better
and live lives that please you in every way,
through Jesus Christ our Lord.
Amen.

Something to ponder

1 Why is it hard for us to conceive of God as happily self-sufficient?
2 What would it be like for us if God was moody and changeable all the time?
3 What *would* God make of your social media engagement?
4 Praise God that he has descended far beneath his loftiness (as Calvin put it) to speak to us in a way we can understand.

2

Why please God?

For this reason, since the day we heard about you, we have not stopped praying for you. We continually ask God to fill you with the knowledge of his will through all the wisdom and understanding that the Spirit gives, so that you may live a life worthy of the Lord and please him in every way: bearing fruit in every good work, growing in the knowledge of God, being strengthened with all power according to his glorious might so that you may have great endurance and patience, and giving joyful thanks to the Father, who has qualified you to share in the inheritance of his holy people in the kingdom of light. For he has rescued us from the dominion of darkness and brought us into the kingdom of the Son he loves, in whom we have redemption, the forgiveness of sins.

(Colossians 1:9–14)

Do you enjoy Christmases? Do you enjoy getting lots of presents, seeing family and friends, and watching the big film on Christmas Day? There's a lot to enjoy at Christmastime and over the New Year holiday. Jesus said it is more blessed to give than to receive (Acts 20:35). We say it's better to give presents than to get them. Although we may not quite believe that completely – I'm always rather pleased with a book token or a big slab of chocolate – there is something in it. It's great to watch other people's faces as they open the presents you've bought for them. Will they love it or hate it? Are they pleased with it or nonplussed? Then (hopefully) to see the delight in their faces and to observe the enjoyment they get out of their gifts.

Don't you wish you could see God's face sometimes? To know what makes him smile? To know what makes him frown? In all our human relationships we have a pretty good idea of what our friends and relatives like. Uncle George doesn't like Brussels sprouts; Aunty Margaret enjoys watching the King's speech; Mum likes to sleep through the midday episode of *EastEnders*; Lee can't stand curry. But what does God like and dislike? What pleases him?

In one of my quiet times alone with God many years ago, I discovered a verse which has come to mean a great deal to me over the years. Ephesians 5:10 says, 'Find out what pleases the Lord'. I took it as a command. That's a good idea, I thought – I should find out what pleases the Lord Jesus, so I can do it. So I did a bit of further study on this and looked up all the verses in the Bible which talk about God being pleased with something or someone, God taking pleasure in something, finding it good or acceptable. Basically, I asked my Bible: what does God delight in, or rejoice over? What makes him smile? And I made a list of all the answers.

It took ages, of course, even with a computer Bible program, because there are hundreds of verses with those words 'please' or 'delight' in – and not all of them refer to God. Masters are pleased with their servants, or not. People are pleased with their kings, or not. Men are pleased with their wives, or not. (There was nothing about being pleased with silly Christmas jumpers.) When you sift through everything, you end up with several pages of material that's of some relevance to what pleases God.

Yet it's not as simple as just compiling a list and then working your way through it to tick off the things it says. I can do this with other lists of likes and dislikes. I know my wife, Kerry, likes flowers – *check*, done that recently. She likes concerts – *check*, took her to one recently. She doesn't like it when I crack my knuckles … well, we'll keep working on this. No, what the Bible says about pleasing God is much more challenging, demanding and life-embracing than a mere list of God's likes and dislikes. I mean, there *are* lists in the Bible, such as the Ten Commandments or the elaboration of the fruit of the Spirit in Galatians 5:22–3. But those are not checklists we can merely work our way through once and be done with. God's word is far more challenging than that.

We can group a lot of what the Bible says about this into a few major categories. This is what we're going to look at in the following chapters. We're going to obey Ephesians 5 and find out what pleases the Lord by looking at this theme as it emerges in various parts of God's word. That means also looking at what it says about God's dislikes too, the things he finds disgusting or abominable – the things he hates.

This is not the sort of thing I usually do when I'm preaching and teaching God's word. Usually, I work through a book of the Bible bit by bit, expounding it as I go. I find that's a great way to organise a sermon series in church, because I'm not clever enough or creative enough to think up my own topics to preach on every week. If I did that, I'd probably only preach on my top ten favourite passages or subjects all the time anyway. So working through the message of Scripture as it presents itself page by page is a really helpful discipline for me, and means I have to engage even with the difficult verses.

Here, we're doing things a little differently. We're still going to be looking at what the Bible says, of course, and letting the word itself shape our thoughts and agenda. But like a beautiful complex crystal, sometimes the Bible only reveals certain things if you look at it from a different angle or stand back from the individual sparkles and look at the whole every once in a while. There's no one book of the Bible given over entirely to the subject of pleasing God; no passage where it's all summed up as the main point in one comprehensive paragraph. Yet there are hundreds of references to it scattered throughout the pages of Scripture, which God has left there for us to mine and gather up, to compare and contrast, and reflect on. As the Puritan theologian John Owen (1616–83) once said:

Many important truths are not clearly delivered in any one singular testimony or proposition in the Scripture, but the mind of God concerning them is to be gathered and learned by comparing of several scriptures, their order and respect unto one another … And one principal way and means of our search is, the comparing together of divers places treating concerning the same matter or truth. This by some is despised, by the most neglected; which causes them to know little and mistake much in the holy things of God.[1]

The purpose of life

Pleasing God is an important theme in the Bible and surfaces all over the place. That's reason enough to dig in and have a look at it. But the biggest reason to explore this whole area is that pleasing God is meant to be the purpose of every Christian's life. As the great Baptist preacher Charles Spurgeon (1834–92) said, 'It should be the aim of every one of us to please God.'[2] Or as the contemporary pastor Rick Warren says in his best-selling book *The Purpose Driven Life*, 'The smile of God is the goal of your life'.[3]

This is the grand purpose statement for my whole life as a Christian. My reason for being here on earth in the first place is to please God. So it is my target, my ambition and the reason I was created. Everything tends towards some end or purpose. Everyone is driven by some ultimate ambition. Some are compelled by the desire for happiness, the pursuit of which is our 'unalienable right' according to the United States Declaration of Independence. As Christians we know, however, that we will only be truly happy when

---

1 John Owen, *An Exposition of the Epistle to the Hebrews* in *The Works of John Owen*, ed. W. H. Goold (Edinburgh: Johnstone & Hunter, 1854), 21:288–9 (on Hebrews 4:5). I have updated the language slightly.

2 C. H. Spurgeon, 'Faith Essential to Pleasing God' in *The Metropolitan Tabernacle Pulpit Sermons* (London: Passmore & Alabaster, 1889), 35:445.

3 Rick Warren, *The Purpose Driven Life* (Grand Rapids, MI: Zondervan, 2002), p. 86.

we see God face to face (1 Corinthians 13:12). There is no true or lasting happiness to be found in anything other than God, whether we try sensual pleasures such as eating, drinking, exercising or sex, or seek happiness in riches, influence or reputation. These are not the highest goals, but only things we use in a forlorn attempt to reach perfect happiness.

One of the most famous summaries of the faith, The Westminster Larger Catechism, encapsulated it in the seventeenth century by saying that 'Man's chief and highest end is to glorify God and fully to enjoy Him forever'. This was getting at the idea that we don't simply use God to attain something else, something better; our ultimate purpose is to enjoy *him* as the highest of all. As St Augustine (354–430), an African bishop in the early church, said:

> to *enjoy* a thing is to rest with satisfaction in it for its own sake. To *use*, on the other hand, is to employ whatever means are at one's disposal to obtain what one desires ... The true objects of enjoyment, then, are the Father and the Son and the Holy Spirit.[4]

In other words, we don't use God: if anything, he uses us. But we can enjoy him.

This is helpful and true. But we could tweak it and make the Catechism even more God-centred. What is humankind's chief and highest end? Our chief and highest end is to glorify God and *be enjoyed by him* forever. I mean this in the sense that, ultimately, we exist for him, not he for us. The universe revolves around him, and our purpose in it all is to give him glory and pleasure. That this will also lead to our own greatest delight and good is a fabulous side-effect of that focused aim, because this is how the universe

---

4 Augustine of Hippo, *On Christian Doctrine* in *St. Augustin's City of God and Christian Doctrine*, ed. P. Schaff, tr. J. F. Shaw (Buffalo, NY: Christian Literature Company, 1887), pp. 523–4 (1.4–5), emphasis added.

was created to work, in harmonious mutual joy. As Paul writes in 1 Corinthians 10:31, 'So whether you eat or drink or whatever you do, do it all for the glory of God.'

This is how we can achieve the highest possible level of human happiness. Yet if we refuse to put God at the centre, and try to live life focused on pleasing ourselves, it always degenerates into selfishness and disaster. We lose our spiritual sensitivity and are corrupted by deceitful desires which promise more than they can ever deliver (see Ephesians 4:17–24). If we persist in that mindset, the ultimate curse is that God will walk away saying, 'Please yourselves' – which we will try and fail to do, to our never-ending regret. Or as the Puritan preacher Thomas Manton (1620–77) so eloquently put it:

> Alas! what a mean spirit have they that drive no higher trade than providing for the flesh, or accommodating a life which must shortly expire! Like foolish birds who, with great art and contrivance, feather a nest, which within a little while they leave. But how divine and god-like are they who look to higher things, to please God, enjoy communion with him, and live with him for ever![5]

But why should we live to please God? The Bible gives me at least three reasons to make this my overarching motivation for everything. We please God because we are different now, because one day we will be judged and because he is our master.

We please God because we are different now

The Bible says that we are to please God because we are different now. If we're Christians, we are transformed. That's the main point of Ephesians 5, the passage which started off my thinking on this

---

5 Thomas Manton, *The Complete Works of Thomas Manton* (London: James Nisbet & Co., 1871), 2:220.

subject. The big point in Ephesians 1 – 3 is that God has a plan to bring all things together under Christ for his own glory (Ephesians 1:10). Believers have been made a part of that plan, and so we are to live in a way which is consistent with his purpose for unity in Christ. That is Paul's point in Ephesians 4. In chapter 5, then, Paul contrasts living in the light of God's strategy with how the world lives, or how we used to live before we became Christians:

Follow God's example, therefore, as dearly loved children and walk in the way of love, just as Christ loved us and gave himself up for us as a fragrant offering and sacrifice to God.

But among you there must not be even a hint of sexual immorality, or of any kind of impurity, or of greed, because these are improper for God's holy people. Nor should there be obscenity, foolish talk or coarse joking, which are out of place, but rather thanksgiving. For of this you can be sure: No immoral, impure or greedy person – such a person is an idolater – has any inheritance in the kingdom of Christ and of God. Let no one deceive you with empty words, for because of such things God's wrath comes on those who are disobedient. Therefore do not be partners with them.

For you were once darkness, but now you are light in the Lord. Live as children of light (for the fruit of the light consists in all goodness, righteousness and truth) and find out what pleases the Lord.

(Ephesians 5:1–10)

It is quite clear from how Paul writes this, that we are meant to be distinctive. So, Ephesians 5 says we are to walk in love (verse 2), not vice (verse 3). Walking in vice, that is, in sexual immorality, impurity and greed, is out of place for us. Indeed, if we persist in such a lifestyle, we have no inheritance in the kingdom of Christ and of God (verse 5). That is, if we worship the god of sex, or the god of shopping – if we are full of lust and acquisitiveness, and only live to satisfy our physical senses – we are worshipping an idol, a false god. We will, consequently, have no place in the kingdom of the one true God.

Since Christians are meant to be different now, we shouldn't live as we used to live when we worshipped those idols. Society may make us feel as if there isn't anything particularly wrong with such a way of life – as if what the Bible says about sex and greed is all just a bit extremist and not to be taken too seriously. But Paul says, in verse 6, 'Let no one deceive you with empty words'. Because God's wrath – his settled, righteous anger – rests on those who live in such disobedience. He anticipates that people will scoff at such an idea, but warns us that it's all too real.

We Christians on the other hand are to be different, because God has changed us. We are light, and so should walk not just in love but as children of light, says Paul. That means living in a way that is good and right and true. And then comes that key verse 10: we are to walk as children of light and try to discern what pleases the Lord Jesus. Actually, it's not two different things in the original: walking in the light and pleasing God. It literally says, 'Walk as children of light … finding out what pleases the Lord.' So the discernment of what pleases the Lord is part and parcel of what it means to live in the light. If we are trying to please him, we are walking as children of light. If we are children of light – if we are different now – then we will naturally be engaged in trying to find out what pleases the Lord.

What does that mean in this context? In the immediate context of Ephesians it means pleasing God rather than pleasing ourselves and indulging our disordered desires (Ephesians 2:1–3; 5:3–5). That's what sexual immorality and greed are all about: gratifying the cravings of our sinful natures and giving ourselves up to the unfulfilling quest for more. Such passionate pursuit of pleasure for ourselves is in direct contrast to a life dedicated to God's pleasure. Do we chase after the idols of personal fulfilment and material security that incur the anger of God if we make them our ultimate goals? Or do we abandon such hollow objectives for a life which God would enjoy instead?

We can abandon such things because the gospel makes us different, and reorientates our desires. As the American preacher John Piper puts it:

> the gospel is the good news that God is the all-satisfying end of all our longings, and that, even though he does not need us, and is in fact estranged from us because of our God-belittling sins, he has, in the great love with which he loved us, made a way for sinners to drink at the river of his delights through Jesus Christ.[6]

If only we could grasp how shallow and unsatisfying our this-worldly desires are, and how fulfilling and pleasurable it can be to sip from this inexhaustible fountain of all good things instead! What a transformative difference it would make in our lives.

Walking in the light and pleasing God also means, in the context of Ephesians 5:11–14, that we are to shine the light of God's truth on every aspect of our lives and every decision we make. Paul says:

> Have nothing to do with the fruitless deeds of darkness, but rather expose them. It is shameful even to mention what the disobedient do in secret. But everything exposed by the light becomes visible – and everything that is illuminated becomes a light.

By shining the light of Christ onto things, we expose whether they are pleasing to God or detestable to him. And if they are good then they will produce the fruit of the light: spiritual photosynthesis if

---

6 John Piper, *The Pleasures of God* (Fearn, Ross-shire: Mentor, 2001), p. 196.

you like. But if they are bad, the light will cause them to shrivel up and die.

What is that light? It's picture language so maybe we're not meant to dissect it too much. But I think the light we expose our lives to has to be something like 'the truth that is in Jesus' (Ephesians 4:21). The gospel, ultimately the whole Bible, as we dwell on it and meditate on it and pray it through, as we bring its teaching to bear on our lives, will show us what is pleasing to God and what is not. Which means we need to know what the whole Bible says on this topic of living to please God! It also means we need to pray, as Paul did in the prayer from Colossians at the start of this chapter, that God will fill us with a knowledge of his will *so that* we can please him.

So the smile of God is the goal of our lives because we are different now. Our lives, if we are Christians, have been reoriented so that we no longer live to please ourselves but to please Jesus, who loved us and gave himself up for us. Ultimately, that means we will enjoy a place in the kingdom of Christ and of God. It is also a wonderfully liberating way to steer our lives on this side of that eternal kingdom. It puts everything else into proper perspective. As Spurgeon once preached, 'The best cure for the cares of this life is to care much to please God. If we loved him better, we should love the world far less, and be less troubled about our portion in it.'[7]

We please God because he is our judge

Pleasing God should also be our aim in life because he is our judge. We can see this very clearly in 2 Corinthians 5:8–10:

> We are confident, I say, and would prefer to be away from the body and at home with the Lord. So we make it our goal to

---

7 Spurgeon, 'Darkness before the Dawn' in *The Metropolitan Tabernacle Pulpit Sermons*, 42:382.

please him, whether we are at home in the body or away from it. For we must all appear before the judgment seat of Christ, so that each of us may receive what is due us for the things done while in the body, whether good or bad.

The apostle Paul says that whatever his personal circumstances are, whether he lives or dies is of no consequence. What matters is that his ambition is fulfilled. And his great aspiration in life is, he says, to please *him*; to please Christ. But notice what motivates him in this longing. It is the thought of judgement day. I want to please Christ, he says, because one day I will appear before him to give an account of my life. Then I will receive what is due to me, depending on what I have done (see also Romans 14:10–12 and verse 18).

So we strive to please Christ now, knowing that a day is coming when his pleasure or displeasure with us will be publicly revealed. A day when the smile of God will be no intangible, ethereal daydream but a concrete reality. Our lives as Christians will be weighed in the balance and we will receive what is due (a thought which should have given Paul's opponents in Corinth great pause for thought). As Paul puts it elsewhere, talking to people whose lot in this life was often hard and difficult:

Whatever you do, work at it with all your heart, as working for the Lord, not for human masters, since you know that you will receive an inheritance from the Lord as a reward. It is the Lord Christ you are serving.
(Colossians 3:23–4)

There will be a delightful reward for good service. 'Jesus invites us to spend eternity with a happy God when he says, "enter into the *joy* of your Master" (Matthew 25:23)', says John Piper.[8] Indeed, God

---

8 Piper, *The Pleasures of God*, p. 26.

himself *is* our very great reward, as he said to Abram (Genesis 15:1). What could be better than knowing him and being united with him in joy forever?

The judgement that Paul is talking about in 2 Corinthians 5 is not the judgement which decides our ultimate fate in heaven or hell. No, the verdict in that sense has already been passed, when *on the cross* we hear the voice of God say, 'Christ is guilty: [*Lee*] is free. Christ is cut off: [*Lee*] is accepted. Christ is condemned: [*Lee*] is pardoned.' (Insert your own name here, believer!) My eternal security rests on the work of Christ in my place, as he bore the punishment that was due to me for my rebellion against God: 'There is now no condemnation for those who are in Christ Jesus' (Romans 8:1). Whoever believes in Jesus 'shall not perish but have eternal life' (John 3:16).

Yet there are, it seems, degrees of reward in eternity.[9] They depend on how I live (and suffer) as a Christian. Just as there are nuanced degrees of punishment for those who reject God (as Jesus asserts in Luke 12:47–8). Paul says 'each of us may receive what is due us for the things done while in the body, whether good or bad' (2 Corinthians 5:10). I don't know what these rewards are exactly. No doubt it's impossible for us to really appreciate what it will be like, with our limited understanding. In the early church, Bishop Irenaeus of Lyon in France (130–200) said, 'The more we have loved him, the more glory shall we receive from him, when we are continually in the presence of the Father.'[10] Whatever these rewards are, they do matter. And they will be fair, related somehow to the good or bad we have done 'in the body' on earth.

---

9 For an alternative view to that presented here, see Craig L. Blomberg, 'Degrees of Reward in the Kingdom of Heaven?' in *Journal of the Evangelical Theology Society* 35/2 (1992), pp. 159–72.

10 Irenaeus of Lyons, 'Irenæus against Heresies', in *The Apostolic Fathers with Justin Martyr and Irenaeus*, ed. A. Roberts, J. Donaldson and A. C. Coxe, vol. 1 of *The Ante-Nicene Fathers* (Buffalo, NY: Christian Literature Company, 1885), p. 478.

This is somewhat mysterious. Jesus talked in his parables about giving people cities to rule, depending on how well they had served him in smaller matters (see the servants who receive ten cities and five cities in Luke 19:17–19). There is something wildly disproportionate in his generosity there, but also something proportional, something fitting about the reward (the servant who looked after five minas got five cities, for example, not three or six). There will be some kind of differentiation, and we will all have a vast variety of different experiences of glory and pleasures in it. It will not be a bland, vanilla experience, identical for each one. At the same time, as Augustine rightly says:

> But who can conceive, not to say describe, what degrees of honor and glory shall be awarded to the various degrees of merit? Yet it cannot be doubted that there shall be degrees. And in that blessed city there shall be this great blessing, that no inferior shall envy any superior, as now the archangels are not envied by the angels, because no one will wish to be what he has not received, though bound in strictest concord with him who has received; as in the body the finger does not seek to be the eye, though both members are harmoniously included in the complete structure of the body. And thus, along with his gift, greater or less, each shall receive this further gift of contentment to desire no more than he has.[11]

So no one will be unhappy and discontent in heaven. Jesus is terrifically generous, and we won't be envious of what he will give to others – we'll be thrilled for them and impressed by the suitableness of what he gives. After all, he has the right to do what he wants with his own gifts. That's the point of his parable in Matthew 20:1–16, where every worker is paid a single denarius regardless of how long

---

11 Augustine, *The City of God* in *St. Augustin's City of God and Christian Doctrine*, p. 510 (22.30.2).

they worked; I don't think it is to say that everyone will get exactly the same reward, except in the sense that heaven itself and being with Jesus is the greatest prize. All those who persistently love and long for Christ's appearing will one day be awarded the crown of life and righteousness (James 1:12; 2 Timothy 4:7). And in his heavenly kingdom, he will honour and make use of us (in all our diversity) as seems best to his judicious wisdom. I don't imagine anyone will question his wise and perfect judgement about how to arrange things in the new creation.

In an absolute sense, none of us deserves a reward anyway; 'all have sinned and fall short of the glory of God' (Romans 3:23). Even when we are converted, our works are imperfect, and Jesus taught us to say, 'We have only done our duty' (Luke 17:10). If we are somehow to 'receive what is due us for the things done while in the body' (2 Corinthians 5:10), it is only because, as Augustine said, 'God crowns his own gifts, not our deservings'.[12] We haven't earned anything by our merits as such. We have nothing to be arrogant or boastful about if we become Christians, resist temptation and diligently persevere to the end in his service. It is all of grace. If, with the constant help of his Spirit, we make good use of the gifts he grants us in this life, and he gives us an appropriate reward for that at the end, the glory is his. But when the time comes, the Bible says he *will* certainly be assessing our use of his gifts and how we have suffered in his service, and be responding accordingly.

Paul links our degree of reward in heaven to the degree to which we have pleased God in this life. He makes it his aim to please God *now*, he says, because – 'for' (2 Corinthians 5:10) – he knows there is a judgement for Christians to face. He is motivated by that future

---

12 Augustine, 'Expositions on the Book of Psalms' in *Saint Augustin: Expositions on the Book of Psalms*, ed. P. Schaff, tr. A. C. Coxe, vol. 8 of *A Select Library of the Nicene and Post-Nicene Fathers of the Christian Church, First Series* (New York, NY: Christian Literature Company, 1888), p. 505 (on Psalm 103:6). See also John Calvin, *Institutes of the Christian Religion*, ed. J. T. McNeill, tr. F. L. Battles (Louisville, KY: Westminster John Knox Press, 2011), 3.18.1–10.

judgement, particularly by the thought of receiving what is due, as our rewards are always according to what we have done (Revelation 22:12; see also Matthew 16:27, 1 Corinthians 3:8, and Ephesians 6:8). Paul wants Christ to enjoy looking back as they sit down together on that day to scrutinise carefully the record of Paul's life and ministry. He doesn't want to see him frown and have to explain himself to the Lord.

We have to be careful at this point. It's not that God saves me by his grace and then expects me to keep myself saved by doing good works and earning my way into a good spot in heaven. No, salvation is by grace and not works. If God has saved me – if I am his – I cannot lose my place in his new creation. It depends on his mercy, not my performance. That being said, my wholeheartedness as a Christian does still matter – emphatically so. He has saved me to walk in good works, 'which God prepared in advance for us to do' (Ephesians 2:10). The mercy of God can all too easily become our excuse for laziness or spiritual drift, and taking God for granted. So as Thomas Manton said, 'Whosoever will live happily with the Lord in glory must have a care to please him in the present life.'[13] I am still responsible for how I live my life. To be justified by grace alone is not a pillow on which to lay my head and sleep, but an engine to drive my glad obedience and diligent service.

This judgement day for Christians is not meant as a blow to our assurance. Paul mentions it as a spur to our commitment, an encouragement to be more dedicated and pleasing to Christ. In the immediate context, it has to do with evangelism. It's because Paul knows that he will appear before the judgement seat of Christ one day to give an account of his life that he uses his time wisely to persuade men and women to turn to God: 'Since, then, we know what it is to fear the Lord, we try to persuade others' (2 Corinthians 5:11). He does this not only because others will have to face

---

13 Manton, *Complete Works*, 14:62.

judgement but because Paul is an evangelist, is suffering because of that, and will be assessed on this basis. We'll come back to this as a motive for evangelism later on in the book.

In all these things, we are not motivated by a 'pay differential', or by any thought of doing better than other Christians, but simply by the thought of pleasing God. So, as American theologian R. C. Sproul (1939–2017) put it, 'Every Christian should have a passion to please God. We are to delight in honoring Him. It should be our greatest desire to please our Redeemer.'[14] Why? Because talk of his pleasure makes us contemplate the reward that he will give to those who serve him well.

We please God because he is our master

Mention of Paul as an evangelist brings me to several other texts on this subject of pleasing God. I found as I trawled through all the passages on this that there is a little group of them on the subject of pleasing God in public ministry. So, before we close this chapter, let's look at what they say. Their main thrust is that we should please God because he is our master.

But just a moment! I was actually expecting to find the Bible telling us to please God because he is our Father, weren't you? Humanly speaking, children often do things to please their parents. But that seems surprisingly absent from the Bible's own way of talking about this subject. The closest I have found to this motivation is Jeremiah 3:19 and Malachi 3:17, although neither of these explicitly mention 'pleasing' the Father, but following him or serving him. Perhaps you can find a text I've missed? I have also been puzzled as to why Scripture doesn't explicitly say our motivation for pleasing God is because we *love* him. Although our love is pleasing to him (Song of Songs 4:10 perhaps), the way the Bible tells it, we *obey* because we love him (e.g. John 14:15), though

---

14 R. C. Sproul, *Pleasing God: Discovering the Meaning and Importance of Sanctification*, 2nd edition (Colorado Springs, CO: David C. Cook, 2012), preface.

obedience is, of course, pleasing to God. It's important to listen to the way God himself actually uses these metaphors in his unerring word, rather than reading our own categories and understandings into them if possible. What the Bible does clearly say, however, is that we should please God because he is our master, our Lord.

At the start of this book, I said the concept of pleasing people comes up in many contexts in the Bible, and not just when talking about pleasing God. One of those contexts is in the dynamic of the relationship between servants and masters, or soldiers and their commanders. To please someone in a biblical sense is not just to be pleasant to them and make them smile, but to do something which serves them and their purposes. So in 2 Timothy 2:4 Paul tells Timothy: 'No one serving as a soldier gets entangled in civilian affairs, but rather tries to please his commanding officer.' This is in the context of Timothy's ministry as a soldier of Christ, passing on the gospel from one generation to the next. The idea is that Timothy should remain at his post and not be swayed in gospel ministry by suffering or difficulty, but continue pleasing his commanding officer, the Lord.[15]

The same idea also comes up in 1 Thessalonians 2, where Paul is defending his own ministry from opponents in the city. In verse 4 he says: 'we speak as those approved by God to be entrusted with the gospel. We are not trying to please people but God, who tests our hearts.' Again we see there must have been a real temptation to please people rather than God, to use flattery or to 'put on a mask to cover up greed' (1 Thessalonians 2:5) while he was there. Yet he asserts that he was never deflected from this goal of pleasing God, because he was a servant of God. That is, he was *approved* by him, it says, and entrusted by him with the gospel. So Paul's pleasing of God was all to do with serving him.

---

15 I've looked at this passage in more detail in Lee Gatiss, *Fulfil Your Ministry: 2 Timothy and Titus and the Challenges of Serving the Gospel* (Fearn, Ross-shire: Christian Focus, 2024), pp. 43–6.

Finally, we turn to Galatians chapter 1. At the start of this letter, Paul issues a stinging rebuke to the Galatians for deserting the gospel (Galatians 1:6). In verses 8 and 9 he says twice that anyone who preaches another gospel should be cursed:

> even if we or an angel from heaven should preach a gospel other than the one we preached to you, let them be under God's curse! As we have already said, so now I say again: If anybody is preaching to you a gospel other than what you accepted, let them be under God's curse!

Now that's a pretty hard thing to say, and not easy for anyone to hear. So, verse 10: 'Am I now trying to win the approval of human beings, or of God? Or am I trying to please people? If I were still trying to please people, I would not be a servant of Christ.'

Notice again the language of approval and pleasing. It is clearly linked to the idea of service, of being a servant of Christ. Paul is saying that obviously he's not trying to win friends and influence people with his harsh denunciation of false teachers. His only concern is to please and serve his master: Christ. Even when that means doing the difficult thing, Paul feels bound to do it, because he is a servant, a bondservant or slave. He's under orders, and must do his master's bidding.

So the common idea in these three texts from 2 Timothy, 1 Thessalonians and Galatians is that Paul is a servant of God and as such his goal is to please his master, to render him good service. This is not advocating slavery as a socio-economic system as such, of course. But it does remind us that the basic Christian confession is that Jesus – not me – is *Lord*.

This is of the utmost importance for all Christians, but especially those who teach and preach the word of God. John Chrysostom (347–407) was one of the best-known and most admired preachers of the early church, and archbishop of Constantinople. Yet he was all too aware of the dangers and temptations of trying to please people rather than God. He wrote: 'Let, therefore, the man who undertakes the strain of teaching never give heed to the good opinion of the outside world, nor be dejected in soul on account of such persons.' Instead, he is to 'labor at his sermons' with a view to pleasing God, 'for let this alone be his rule and determination, in discharging this best kind of workmanship, not acclamation, nor good opinions'. It may happen that a good preacher will receive some positive feedback. So, says Chrysostom, if people do praise the preacher, the preacher should not refuse to accept their praise. However, at the same time, 'when his hearers do not offer this, let him not seek it, let him not be grieved'. It should be 'a sufficient consolation in his labors, and one greater than all', he said, when the preacher is able 'to be conscious of arranging and ordering his teaching with a view to pleasing God'.[16]

The prolific Puritan preacher Richard Baxter of Kidderminster (1615–91) also warned his fellow ministers against pride in the pulpit. When I first started preaching, I had this text pinned up in my study as a necessary reminder:

And when pride has made the sermon, it goes with us into the pulpit; it forms our tone, it animates us in the delivery, it takes us off from that which may be displeasing, however necessary, and sets us in pursuit of vain applause. In short, the sum of all this is, it makes men, both in studying and preaching, to seek themselves, and deny God, when they should seek God's glory and deny themselves. When they should ask, 'What shall I say, and how shall I say it,' to please God best, and do most good? Instead, it makes them ask: 'What shall I say, and

---

16 John Chrysostom, *Treatise Concerning the Christian Priesthood* in *Saint Chrysostom: On the Priesthood, Ascetic Treatises, Select Homilies and Letters, Homilies on the Statutes*, ed. P. Schaff, tr. W. R. W. Stephens (New York, NY: Christian Literature Company, 1889), 9:72–3.

how shall I deliver the message to be thought a learned able preacher, and to be applauded by all who hear me?' When the sermon is done, pride goes home with them, and makes them more eager to know whether they were applauded, than whether they did prevail for the saving of souls! Were it not for shame, they could find in their hearts to ask people, how they liked them, and to draw out their commendation. If they perceive that they are highly thought of, they rejoice, as having attained their end; but if they perceive that they are esteemed but weak or common men, they are displeased, as having missed the prize they had in view.[17]

This is not necessarily the best approach if our aim in ministry is to be popular. Martin Luther warned his fellow preachers that

because we try to please God and not men, we bring upon ourselves the envy of the devil and of hell itself. We bear the slanders and curses of the world, death, and every evil. Thus Paul says here: 'I do not try to please men so that they will praise my doctrine and call me an outstanding teacher. I want to please only God. Whoever tries to please God will have men as his bitter enemies.'[18]

If we're pleasing God, whether we are apostles or preachers or not, we should expect opposition. The trouble is, preachers are often not content with pleasing God, but we try instead to please those who pay our way, giving them what their 'itching ears want to hear' (2 Timothy 4:3). This can involve a degree of self-censorship: never touching the sore spots in the congregation or the culture, for fear

---

17 Richard Baxter, *The Practical Works of the Rev. Richard Baxter*, ed. W. Orme (London: James Duncan, 1830), 14:155 (from *The Reformed Pastor* (1656)).

18 Martin Luther, *Luther's Works*, ed. J. J. Pelikan, H. C. Oswald and H. T. Lehmann (St Louis, MO: Concordia, 1999), 26:60.

of what people will say or do to us. We ought to be more concerned with what God will say and do about this on judgement day.

The same is true for all of us. Christ is our Lord, our Master. So our life is not our own. We belong to another and must do his bidding regardless of cultural pressures. We are not apostles like Paul, of course, but our goal is to please God in whatever he has given us to do. Clearly there will be temptations, to please ourselves or to please other people – to do what will earn applause, gratitude or a good name, instead of focusing on what will please our Lord and enhance *his* reputation. But the smile of God is worth more than the approval of others. As Spurgeon put it, 'We cannot spend our lives in seeking the smiles of men, for pleasing God is the one object we pursue.'[19] So we must always ask ourselves, as he did, 'Is it my master-motive to please God?'[20] Can we assert, as Jesus himself did, 'I seek not to please myself but him who sent me' (John 5:30)?

There's a great story of a young violin player. She was a child prodigy and was taught by the famous violinist, Sir Yehudi Menuhin. At her first major concert she played brilliantly and received a rapturous standing ovation from the audience. From the stalls to the balcony, all were impressed. But she didn't react to this lavish praise at all. She wasn't interested in what the crowd thought. As the applause went on and on, she remained emotionless on stage. Then she looked up to the royal box to see Yehudi Menuhin himself, her teacher and 'master'. What did *he* think? He caught her eye and he just nodded and smiled. A huge grin broke across her face! She was only interested in pleasing him.

That's what we need to dwell on as followers of Jesus. Are we the same as that young girl? Are we only interested in pleasing our

---

19 Spurgeon, 'Man, Whose Breath Is in His Nostrils' in *The Metropolitan Tabernacle Pulpit Sermons*, 33:538.

20 Spurgeon, 'What Is the Verdict?' in *The Metropolitan Tabernacle Pulpit Sermons*, 31:448.

master, or are we playing to the crowd as Christians, and trying to earn other people's applause?

The Bible encourages us to put God first. To be more interested in what he thinks than in what anybody else might say. Because he is our master. Because one day we will be judged. And because we are meant to be different now. So let's resolve to *be* different, to let God be first in our hearts, and to make it our ambition to please him in every way. Let's find out what pleases him, and do it with all our hearts.

Prayer

Almighty God,
whose Son Jesus Christ sought to please you in everything:
Grant us grace, by your Holy Spirit,
so to focus on the things of heaven in our daily routines
that we will live in the light of eternity
and the crown of righteousness that awaits us there,
through the merits of Jesus Christ our Saviour.
Amen.

Something to ponder

1 Is the goal of your life to please God, or to be happy? How can you tell?
2 Think about the ways your life is distinctive as a Christian. Are there areas where it is not, but perhaps should be?
3 How much does the thought of a future day of judgement motivate you in your daily life?
4 Praise God for how he is changing you.

3

Who pleases God?

These are the ones I look on with favor:
 those who are humble and contrite in spirit,
 and who tremble at my word.
(Isaiah 66:2)

Martin Luther once said: 'What is right, that is, what pleases God, should be more important than wealth, body, honor and friends, grace, and enjoyment; and in this case there is no respecting of persons, but only of God.'[1] This should be our number-one priority in life, so that we might glorify God and be enjoyed by him who made us and saved us for himself. So here we are, trying to 'find out what pleases the Lord' as Ephesians 5:10 tells us. The only way we can do that is to ask God himself, which means interrogating his word, the Bible, for answers. As the Covent Garden Puritan Thomas Manton put it, 'Whoever will please God in all things, and will purge his own soul and his life from sin, must take the word of God for his rule and direction.'[2]

So what does the Bible say about *who* pleases God? Is pleasing God something that anybody can do? Can we just wake up one morning and choose to please God? Looking at my large collection of Bible passages on the subject, the answer to that seems to be 'no'. This is rather surprising. The Bible says that some people cannot please God.

---

1 Martin Luther, *Luther's Works*, ed. J. J. Pelikan, H. C. Oswald and H. T. Lehmann (St Louis, MO: Concordia, 1999), 46:132.
2 Thomas Manton, *The Complete Works of Thomas Manton* (London: James Nisbet & Co., 1872), 8:384.

Some people cannot please God

We are familiar with the idea that some people *don't* please God. Clearly he is not pleased when people reject him. He cannot be happy when people decide they will have nothing to do with him or his Son, Jesus Christ. So some people don't please God.

We're also familiar with the idea that some people *don't want* to please God. They reject all thoughts of living their lives to please someone else, especially God. They have their own ideas about what makes a fulfilling and satisfying life, and focusing on someone else's happiness is not it.

Perhaps you feel like that, at least some of the time. You don't want to please God. Perhaps your default creed is more like that of the American Declaration of Independence, which asserts that we all have an 'unalienable right' to 'life, liberty, and the pursuit of happiness' – our *own* happiness, that is. If something or someone prevents us from being happy, then it's our duty to throw off such a hindrance. That's what the American colonies did with King George III on 4 July 1776. They rejected his authority and his right to rule over them. Perhaps we would have done the same with a supposed tyrant like that. Yet this is what many people have also done with God, who is not a tyrant at all, but a loving heavenly Father. We don't want to please him or enthrone him. We certainly don't want to let him decide the important things in our lives. We want to pursue our own ends, and our own definitions of 'life, liberty, and happiness'.

We're familiar with these ideas: some people *don't* please God; some people *don't want* to please God. The Bible, however, goes much further, and says something even more radical and shocking. It says some people *cannot* please God. To see that, let's turn to Romans 8:

Those who live according to the flesh have their minds set on what the flesh desires; but those who live in accordance with the Spirit have their minds set on what the Spirit desires. The mind governed by the flesh is death, but the mind governed by the Spirit is life and peace. The mind governed by the flesh is hostile to God; it does not submit to God's law, nor can it do so. Those who are in the realm of the flesh cannot please God. (Romans 8:5–8)

We're jumping into the middle of a complex argument; chapter 8 of a long letter. But the main points are pretty clear. The apostle Paul is saying there are only two ways to live. We can live according to the flesh or according to the Spirit. 'The flesh' is Paul's way of describing our own internal desires and appetites which seek our own happiness rather than God's. It's our 'sinful nature', not just our literal flesh or skin, but our personal drive, our animating force. If that is what rules our lives, we will set our minds on the things that please it, such as gossip, greed and any form of selfishness, basically. Pleasing the flesh is pleasing ourselves.

Paul says this leads to death. Why? Because the flesh is hostile to God. It is a rival authority. It wants to depose God as king and set itself up as president, judge and lawmaker. Hostility to God equals not submitting to his law, but throwing off his rule and instead pursuing our own form of independent self-government. While that may have been defensible against George III, it is much more serious when the one we seek to topple from his throne is the source of all life and goodness in the universe. To cut ourselves off from *him* is far more dangerous. Not just because we can't live without him – we owe him every breath we take – but because he also has the power to enforce the death sentence for rebels.

Notice that Paul goes further than saying those who live according to the flesh do not submit to God. He says they *cannot* please God. They are unable to submit to God's law. Can't obey, won't obey. Our ancestors Adam and Eve rebelled, and we're stuck in that rebellious state, from the moment we're conceived. We cannot undo their unilateral declaration of independence ourselves. There's no going back. Don't get me wrong – there *is* a very definite way out, via the cross, and the transforming work of God himself within us, giving us a new orientation in life. Yet this is not something we can whip up within ourselves somehow. Once we as a race went down that road, we lost the ability to alter course. Humanly speaking, it's a one-way street. We read in Romans 8 that we are incapable of pleasing God if we are not Christians, if we are not those who set their minds on the things of the Spirit.

The Bible says that it is impossible for someone who is not a believer to please God. Indeed, the gospel says that whoever rejects Jesus 'will not see life, for God's wrath remains on them' (John 3:36). As the theologian John Calvin explains, 'Death hangs over all unbelievers, and keeps them oppressed and overwhelmed in such a manner that they can never escape.'[3] There is nothing, therefore, that someone who remains controlled by the flesh can do to bring a smile to God's face. Nothing. Even if they do very good and noble things in our eyes – give to the poor, work for a charity, undertake great feats of fundraising – none of these things gives God any pleasure if our hearts and minds are set against him. Even our most splendid works are incapable of lifting the wrath of God from our shoulders. Proverbs 15:8 says that 'the LORD detests the sacrifice of the wicked, but the prayer of the upright pleases him'. As Luther explains, 'When the heart is impure and unbelieving, works do not please God, no matter how magnificent they are.'[4]

No good without God

In the NBC 2016 comedy, *The Good Place*, the positive afterlife is presented as a reward given to those who rack up sufficient points

---

3   John Calvin, *Calvin's Commentaries: Volume XVII*, tr. William Pringle (Grand Rapids, MI: Baker, 1993), 2:142 (on John 3:36).

4   Luther, *Luther's Works*, 19:25; cf. 33:176. See also John Calvin, *Institutes of the Christian Religion*, ed. J. T. McNeill, tr. F. L. Battles (Louisville, KY: Westminster John Knox Press, 2011), 3.14.8.

awarded for good deeds in their lifetimes. This is how many, if not most, people think: if my good points outweigh my bad ones, surely God will be pleased? Yet, it seems from his word, he is not. As Gregory the Great (a good theologian who served as bishop of Rome from the sixth century) explained, 'For indeed in the judgment of Almighty God it is not what is given, but by whom it is given, that is regarded.'[5] That is, God cares more about your soul than what you do with your money. So no matter how much you think you have to offer, God doesn't care if he can't have *you*.

This is not how we tend to think. Imagine twins: one is a believer and the other is not. They both do the same good work or noble deed, make identical huge donations to charity, and work to eradicate poverty, war and injustice. We tend to think that God will be equally pleased with both of them, don't we? But according to the Bible, he's not. Because those who are not believers *cannot* please him. Hebrews agrees with Romans: 'without faith it is *impossible* to please God' (Hebrews 11:6, emphasis added). Or as Paul says in Romans 14:23, 'Whatever does not proceed from faith is sin' (ESV). That is, whatever we do, if it is not done out of a loving faithful trust in God, to please him, then it is counted by God as sin; it is repugnant, distasteful, rotten to him. However righteous and virtuous it might look to human eyes, anything which does not spring from a heart that believes and trusts in God cannot be good, because it is not done for the glory of God. It may have good consequences in this world, but then God is an expert at bringing good out of evil.

So if you're living in the 'United States of Me' then be aware that nothing you do will please God. We give him absolutely no pleasure at all in anything we do while we remain in a state of enmity and hostility towards him. It is only when we become part of the 'United Kingdom of God', and submit to him, that we can gain his approval

---

5 Gregory the Great, *Selected Epistles of Gregory the Great, Bishop of Rome (Books IX–XIV)* in *Gregory the Great (Part II), Ephraim Syrus, Aphrahat*, ed. P. Schaff and H. Wace, tr. J. Barmby (New York, NY: Christian Literature Company, 1898), 13:35.

and praise. 'Seek first his kingdom', said Jesus (Matthew 6:33). We can do no good without God. As Charles Spurgeon preached:

> As the man is, such is his work. The stream is of the nature of the spring from which it flows. He who is a rebel, outlawed and proclaimed, cannot gratify his prince by any fashion of service; he must first submit himself to the law. All the actions of rebels are acts done in rebellion. We must first be reconciled to God, or it is a mockery to bring an offering to his altar.[6]

Or as he puts it elsewhere:

> Virtues, in unregenerate men, are nothing but whitewashed sins. The best performance of an unchanged character is worthless in God's sight. It lacks the stamp of grace upon it; and that which has not the stamp of grace is false coin. Be it ever so beautiful in model and finish, it is not what it should be.[7]

Spurgeon also speaks of virtues without faith being merely 'gilded disobedience'.[8] There is nothing wrong with morality. We need all the honesty, faithfulness, sobriety, generosity, kindness and truthfulness that we can get these days. Human life is better for

---

6 C. H. Spurgeon, 'Faith Essential to Pleasing God' in *The Metropolitan Tabernacle Pulpit Sermons* (London: Passmore & Alabaster, 1889), 35:447. See also George Whitefield, who preached, 'My dear friends, what is there in our performances to recommend us unto God? Our persons are in an unjustified state by nature, we deserve to be damned ten thousand times over. And what must our performances be? We can do no good thing by nature. "They that are in the flesh cannot please God" [Romans 8:8]. You may do many things materially good but you cannot do a thing formally and rightly good because nature cannot act above itself. It is impossible that a man who is unconverted can act for the glory of God. He cannot do anything in faith and "whatsoever is not of faith is sin" [Romans 14:23].' Lee Gatiss (ed.), *The Sermons of George Whitefield*, vol. 2 (Wheaton, IL: Crossway, 2012), p. 429.

7 Spurgeon, 'The Search after Happiness' in *The Metropolitan Tabernacle Pulpit Sermons*, 54:396. This was a common theme in Spurgeon's evangelical preaching; see also 12:614–15; 13:548, 632; 31:223; 43:183; 57:299; 59:599–600.

8 C. H. Spurgeon, 'The Sin of Unbelief' in *The New Park Street Pulpit Sermons* (London: Passmore & Alabaster, 1855), 1:20–1.

them. But we need to realise that they do not impress God if we remain estranged from him. They are like slapping God in the face with expensive handmade, silk-lined, leather gloves instead of worn-out woollen mittens. The main thing is, you're still slapping God in the face! As Augustine put it, 'The entire life of unbelievers is a sin, and nothing is good without the highest good. Where the acknowledgment of eternal truth is lacking, there is false virtue, even with the best of morals.'[9]

You may win a Nobel Prize or worldly plaudits with such virtue; but you'll never win the smile of God. Good works without true faith may bring you outward approval, prosperity or inward calmness of mind in this life, but in the life to come, all they earn an unbeliever is what the theologian John Owen calls 'a diminution of the degrees of their torments – they shall not be beaten with so many stripes'[10] – alluding to what Jesus himself says in Luke 12:48. All human works are imperfect, but outside of Christ there is no forgiveness for those imperfections. The eighteenth-century hymn-writer Augustus Montague Toplady (1740–78) wrote in one of his poems:

Jesus, I know full well,
    What my best actions are:
They'd sink my grievous soul to hell,
    If unrefin'd they were.[11]

So that's my first point. Some people cannot please God. They may seemingly have virtue, but as far as God is concerned it is

---

9 Augustine as quoted in Prosper of Aquitaine, *Sententiae ex Augustino Delibatae*, n106, as referenced and translated in Peter Lombard, *The Sentences, book 2: On Creation*, tr. Giulio Silano (Toronto: Pontifical Institute of Mediaeval Studies, 2008), p. 203 (Distinction XLI, Chapter 1.3 (253)).

10 John Owen, *The Works of John Owen*, ed. W. H. Goold (Edinburgh: Johnstone & Hunter, 1854), 10:112.

11 Augustus Montague Toplady, *The Works of Augustus M. Toplady* (London: William Baynes & Son, 1825), 6:334 (poem XXXIV).

false virtue or counterfeit morality. He is not delighted with such offerings. As Toplady put it elsewhere, 'If God hath not wrought living faith in your heart, you have never performed one truly good work in your whole life.'[12]

A dismal doctrine?

I was once told rather curtly that this was a dismal doctrine, because it supposedly left Christians with nothing to say to the world about ethics. When people say such dismissive things, I do try and re-examine what I've said to provoke such a reaction, to see if there's anything in it and whether I'm wrong. That's why I've quoted a few other theologians in this chapter, because I did a deep dive into Christian thinking on this subject to check I wasn't saying something totally barmy or novel here. As I did that, I found this other person's knowledge of Romans 8 and historical theology to be depressingly lacking, but I glory in his dismissal anyway. After all, it is not the Church's job to teach the world to have better morals; rather, Christians point the world to Jesus, who alone can forgive us for our desperate failures to live up to even our own standards. The first thing we need to say to the world about ethics is 'Repent and believe the good news!' (Mark 1:15).

Besides, this is not just my personal interpretation of Romans 8:8, Romans 14:23 and Hebrews 11:6. It's not even simply the private teaching of all the theologians I've just quoted in this section. My

---

12 Toplady, *Works*, 3:12. I also like what Richard Baxter says on this: 'that is formally no good work, which is not intended chiefly to please God ... Moreover, the misery of the unconverted doth further appear in this; that while men are unconverted, nothing that they do can truly please God. There are many works which, for the matter of them, are commanded, which such men may do, but yet there are so many defects, and so much of the venom of their corruption mixt in them, that God hath no delight in them, but doth abhor them ... No man's works please God out of Christ, both because they are unsound and bad in the spring and end, and because their faultiness is not pardoned. But in Christ, the persons and duties of the godly are pleasing to God, because they have his image, and are sincerely good, and because their former sins, and present imperfections are forgiven for the sake of Christ.' Richard Baxter, *The Practical Works of the Rev. Richard Baxter*, ed. W. Orme (London: James Duncan, 1830), 6:106; 7:174; 12:346.

friend's own (and my) denomination publicly professes these biblical truths about what is and is not 'pleasant to God'. The Church of England's doctrinal confession (the Thirty-nine Articles) states that 'we have no power to do good works pleasant and acceptable to God' without God's grace going before us first. It also says:

> Works done before the grace of Christ, and the Inspiration of his Spirit, are not pleasant to God, forasmuch as they spring not of faith in Jesus Christ … yea rather, for that they are not done as God hath willed and commanded them to be done, we doubt not but they have the nature of sin.[13]

The Anglican Homilies, official sermons which express Anglican doctrine in homiletical form, use an arresting image to get this across. They reflect the common teaching of the early, medieval and Reformation church when they say that all the good works of those who do not have faith in Christ 'are like the course of a horse that runs out of the track, which makes a great effort, but to no purpose'.[14] If you ignore Jesus, everything else you do is ultimately a waste of time.

But some people can please God

Yet the picture is not all bleak! There are several people in the Bible who *are* said to please God. In fact, he is *delighted* with them, we're

---

13 Articles 10 and 13 of the Thirty-nine Articles of Religion of the Church of England, on which see Lee Gatiss (ed.), *Foundations of Faith: Reflections on the Thirty-nine Articles* (London: Lost Coin, 2018).

14 Lee Gatiss (ed.), *The First Book of Homilies: The Church of England's Official Sermons in Modern English* (London: Lost Coin, 2021), p. 82, alluding to Augustine's second exposition of Psalm 32:1 in E. B. Pusey (ed.), *Expositions on the Book of Psalms by S. Augustine* (Oxford, 1839), 1:281. Cf. *The Glossa Ordinaria on Romans*, tr. Michael Scott Woodward (Kalamazoo, MI: Medieval Institute Publications, 2011), p. 211 (on Romans 14:23), and Lombard, *Sentences*, 2.40.1.2 in *The Sentences, book 2: On Creation*, tr. Silano, p. 198.

told in some places. So let's have a brief look at who these people are. Who pleases God? First, God is delighted with his chosen people.

God's chosen people

There are quite a few passages where God declares his love for and pleasure in his people. For example, in Psalm 149, the people of Israel are told to praise God's name:

> For the LORD *takes delight* in his people;
>   he crowns the humble with victory.
> Let his faithful people rejoice in this honour
>   and sing for joy on their beds.
> (Psalm 149:4–5, emphasis added)

God takes pleasure in his people, as they praise him for being their God and king. This is a huge boost to our true sense of self-esteem for the believer: God delights in us, so we can sing with awestruck joy at such a privilege. A little further back, we also find Psalm 44, a prayer to God for help in a difficult time for God's people. And the psalmist reminds God that when he saved his people in the past:

> It was not by their sword that they won the land,
>   nor did their arm bring them victory;
> it was your right hand, your arm,
>   and the light of your face, *for you loved them.*
> (Psalm 44:3, emphasis added)

Literally, the last bit there says 'for you delighted in them' (ESV) or were pleased with them. God gave victory to his people not because they were so strong and mighty ('by their own sword', ESV) but simply because he was delighted with them. So the Lord takes pleasure in his people now, and he did in the past when he saved them. Isaiah 62:3–5 also tells us that he will forever delight in his people:

You will be a crown of splendor in the LORD's hand,
    a royal diadem in the hand of your God.
No longer will they call you Deserted,
    or name your land Desolate.
But you will be called Hephzibah,
    and your land Beulah;
for the LORD will *take delight in you*,
    and your land will be married.
As a young man marries a young woman,
    so will your Builder marry you;
as a bridegroom rejoices over his bride,
    so will your God *rejoice over you*.
(emphasis added)

What a beautiful picture! God delighting and revelling in and enjoying his people. Not because of anything they do, but simply because they are his. He rejoices over his people with singing, according to Zephaniah 3:17! And he is no racist God, with a preference for one colour or ethnicity. He accepts, or is pleased with, anyone from anywhere who believes and trusts in him. For, 'God does not show favoritism but accepts from every nation the one who fears him and does what is right' (Acts 10:34–5).

God's chosen king

It slowly emerges throughout the Bible that there is a figure that God is pleased with, within his people. He is especially pleased with his king, in particular with King David and his house. So David says in 1 Chronicles 28:4 (emphasis added):

the LORD, the God of Israel, chose me from my whole family to be king over Israel forever. He chose Judah as leader, and from the tribe of Judah he chose my family, and from my father's sons he was *pleased* to make me king over all Israel.

43

We should note in passing what an interesting use of the language of 'pleasing' this is. God is pleased with his own actions. He made David into a king, and this pleased him, just as Jesus said: 'Do not be afraid, little flock, for your Father has been pleased to give you the kingdom' (Luke 12:32). God is always happy with himself. Whatever he does, he does it because it pleases him. Psalm 135:6 says that 'the LORD does whatever pleases him'. Unlike us, he is perfectly happy with all his decisions and his actions. He is 'the blessed God' (1 Timothy 1:11), literally, the happy God.

The blessed God took pleasure in making David king. Then in 1 Kings 10, we hear the Queen of Sheba say to David's son, King Solomon:

> How happy your people must be! How happy your officials, who continually stand before you and hear your wisdom! Praise be to the LORD your God, *who has delighted in you* and placed you on the throne of Israel. Because of the LORD's eternal love for Israel, he has made you king to maintain justice and righteousness.
> (1 Kings 10:8–9, emphasis added)

God took pleasure in making David king, and he also delighted in Solomon, his son. Indeed, 1 Chronicles 17:27 says that God was pleased to bless the whole house of David, that is, his dynasty; his kingly line. This, it seems, made the Queen of Sheba happy, and ought to have gladdened the hearts of all Solomon's people and officials. Because God's pleasure in making him king was an overspill from the happy heart of God himself, motivated by his plan of eternal love towards his people. This always ripples out in ever-increasing circles as people are caught up in it.

God's servant

In the Old Testament, there is another individual who is also enjoyed by God. That is his servant. That title 'servant of God' is given to a few select individuals in the Old Testament, such as Moses and David. But in Isaiah 42 it is someone else, a unique individual:

> Here is my servant, whom I uphold,
>   my chosen one *in whom I delight;*
> I will put my Spirit on him,
>   and he will bring justice to the nations.
> (Isaiah 42:1, emphasis added)

The identity and role of this special, Spirit-anointed servant of the Lord is made clearer as this central section of Isaiah unfolds. He has come to bring justice, not breaking a bruised reed or snuffing out a smouldering wick (Isaiah 42:3). He is to be a light, not just for Old Testament Israel, but for the Gentiles too in every nation (Isaiah 42:6). He is the servant who will 'display my splendor', God says (Isaiah 49:3), and bring salvation 'to the ends of the earth' (Isaiah 49:6). He will act wisely, and yet people will be appalled by his disfigurement (Isaiah 52:13–14) and the way he is despised and rejected (Isaiah 53:3) – not just by people, but even for a moment by God himself. Isaiah 53:9–10 literally says: 'though he had done no violence, nor was any deceit in his mouth. Yet *the LORD delighted* to crush him and cause him to suffer' (emphasis added).

So from being the one in whom God's soul takes pleasure in Isaiah 42, he becomes the servant whom God is pleased to crush. God is pleased with his servant, and then he is somehow delighted by his death. How can this be? Or rather, *who* can this be? Of course, it is none other than his Son, the Lord Jesus. In everything he did he pleased God his Father. The Spirit of the Lord rested on him. We see this several times in the New Testament. The most striking place is at Jesus' baptism at the beginning of the gospel story. As he comes up from the water, Luke tells us, in a wonderfully Trinitarian verse, 'the Holy Spirit descended on him in bodily form like a dove. And a voice came from heaven: "You are my Son, whom I love; with you I am well pleased"' (Luke 3:22).

They acted together: God the Father who spoke, God the Son who served, and God the Holy Spirit planned that Jesus would die. He was loved by God and always pleased him. Yet he would die for wicked, rebellious human beings like us. He in whom all the fullness of God was pleased to dwell, who always did the things that are pleasing to God, was crushed by the will of God: 'he was pierced for our transgressions, he was crushed for our iniquities; the punishment that brought us peace was on him, and by his wounds we are healed' (Isaiah 53:5).

It seems strange to say it, but Jesus' death brought delight to God. Not the delight of a sadistic monster who loves to see pain inflicted on others. No, God is no sadist. He was not pleased that this was necessary, or happy that his beloved Son should have to suffer. But he was delighted with the obedient humility of his Son, and the outcome of his debased humiliation on the cross. Together they had devised a way to rescue sinful human beings from the deathly consequences of their rebellion, as Jesus voluntarily took the punishment due to our sin upon himself. So that those who did not please God and could not please God might be saved, by the death of the one who did please God in every single way. He gave up his own life, liberty and happiness for the joy of his Father, and our salvation.

So who can please God? Those who reject him and do not trust him, who live to please their own sinful nature, do not please him. But he is delighted with his chosen people, his chosen king, his chosen servant and above all his Son.

Believers can please God

Finally, let's take a look at Hebrews 10 and 11. Here we learn that believers can please God, that is, those who have faith in him:

> By faith Enoch was taken up so that he should not see death, and he was not found, because God had taken him. Now before he was taken he was commended as having pleased God. And without faith it is impossible to please him, for whoever would draw near to God must believe that he exists and that he rewards those who seek him.
> (Hebrews 11:5–6 ESV)

The chapter begins by telling us that by faith the people of old received their commendation from God. Their faith, that is, their trusting obedience or loving loyalty towards God, pleased him. And as we have already seen, without such faith it is impossible to please God.

Why? Because unless we put down our arms and end hostilities with God, unless we give up the pursuit of what Hebrews 11:25 calls 'the fleeting pleasures of sin' and follow him instead, God can never smile on us. Charles Spurgeon asks:

> Is it not strange that the eternal God can ever be 'pleased' with us? It is a wonderful thing, certainly, that we poor creatures should, by any means, be able to give pleasure to the infinitely-happy God; yet so we do when we trust him.[15]

You don't have to do anything extraordinarily amazing. You just have to trust him.

But why is the writer reminding the Hebrew Christians about this? To be sure, he wants to encourage this same faith in his hearers. He wants them too to please God. But there's more to it than that. The context of chapter 10 helps sharpen it further. Hebrews 10:32 says that the people used to be wholehearted, all out for pleasing God every day, in those 'former days'. They joyfully accepted persecution, because they trusted God. But now they are

---

15 Spurgeon, 'Faith without Sight' in *The Metropolitan Tabernacle Pulpit Sermons*, 47:164.

tempted – tempted to throw it all away, and lose their reward. The writer is encouraging them to endurance in the face of persecution.

Hebrews urges perseverance for two reasons. First, because it is good for the Hebrew Christians. Hebrews 10 tells us that there is great reward in living a life of faith and trusting God. Verse 39 says it is how we preserve our souls (ESV). Second, the writer quotes from Habakkuk, in the Old Testament. Habakkuk's message is one of assurance of God's ultimate intervention in history and a call for fidelity in the meantime. While we wait, we must trust God: 'My righteous one will live by faith' (Hebrews 10:38). But if such a person shrinks back, Hebrews adds, God has *no pleasure* in them. The word in Hebrews 10:39 for 'shrink back' conjures up the picture of those who hesitate to come forward or speak up when they should.

So this is a word for the half-hearted Christian. The righteous live by faith and are rewarded by God, but the reluctant give him no pleasure. God is pleased with those who live by faith, but he is not happy with those who slide backwards or who restrain themselves from wholehearted commitment. Believers actually *can* please God. So the challenge is: *will* you? Since you can, why would you not want to?

It may be simpler to be zealous when you're young or a new Christian perhaps. But I've found as I get older and have more responsibilities that it is much easier for me to worry more about my earthly security and cheerfulness than it is to live every moment for the higher purpose of bringing God pleasure. Sometimes in my weakness, I lose spiritual concentration or simply can't be bothered to ask what God thinks. Then, I almost hear God ask: 'Is that thing you're doing for *me*, Lee, or just for your benefit?' As Thomas Manton says, 'So foolish is that Christian who is earnest for comfort, but taketh no care how to be directed and enabled to please God.'[16] This is a rebuke to my slothful ease.

---

16 Manton, *Complete Works*, 3:294.

Imagine the look on God's face if we care so little about this. 'A frown or an angry look from God, whom the Saint so dearly loves, must needs go near the heart', said the East Anglican pastor William Gurnall (1617–69).[17] Recommit yourself to pleasing God, because as Gurnall's contemporary, Thomas Watson (1620–86), puts it:

The snow covers many a dunghill. A snowy white profession [of faith] covers many a foul heart! The sins of professors [those who profess faith] are more odious. Thistles are bad in a field – but worse in a garden. The sins of the wicked anger God – but the sins of professing Christians grieve him.[18]

It is reassuring that even though a Christian may grieve God's heart by their sin, this is covered by the blood of Christ. There is ample forgiveness if only we return to God with all our heart, mind, soul and strength. The wonderfully pithy Puritan statement, the Westminster Confession of Faith (1647), puts it so well:

God does continue to forgive the sins of those that are justified; and although they can never fall from the state of justification, yet they may, by their sins, fall under God's fatherly displeasure, and not have the light of his countenance restored unto them, until they humble themselves, confess their sins, beg pardon, and renew their faith and repentance.

In the film *Chariots of Fire*, the Christian runner, Eric Liddle, says that God made him fast, and when he ran he felt God's pleasure.[19] Even

---

17 William Gurnall, *The Christian in Compleat Armour*, 3rd edition (London, 1658), 1:144.

18 Thomas Watson, *Religion Our True Interest* (London, 1682), pp. 24–5.

19 *Chariots of Fire*, directed by Hugh Hudson, written by Colin Welland (1981; Burbank, CA: Warner Home Video, 2004).

something as apparently mundane as running can be done to God's pleasure if we are using our God-given abilities for his glory. Psalm 147:10 says, 'His pleasure is *not* in the strength of the horse, nor his delight in the legs of the warrior' (emphasis added). But verse 11 adds that 'the LORD delights in those who fear him, who put their hope in his unfailing love'. So let's love him and trust him, in all that we do, whether that's running in the Olympics or looking after our family. For we know that if we do, God delights in us. As Calvin beautifully summarised it, 'He accepts our service as a father accepts his child's attempt to please him; they are far from perfect and amount to nothing, yet the father is content because he loves his child.'[20]

Christians *can* please God because, as we saw in the Romans 8 passage, we have the Spirit of Christ within us causing us to will and to act for his good pleasure. How sad, then, if those of us who *can* please God choose not to do so, but instead shrink back and are unenthusiastic, weak or feeble in our pursuit of God's pleasure.

Prayer

Almighty God,
the strength of all who put their trust in you:
Since through the weakness of our mortal nature,
we can do nothing good without you,
grant us the help of your grace,
that in keeping your commandments
we may please you both in will and deed,
through Jesus Christ our Lord.
Amen.[21]

---

20 John Calvin, *Sermons on 2 Timothy*, tr. Robert White (Edinburgh: Banner of Truth, 2018), p. 413 (on 2 Timothy 4:7–8, citing Psalm 103:13).

21 The Collect for the first Sunday after Trinity in the 1662 Book of Common Prayer. Updated language version from Lee Gatiss (ed.), *Gathering Our Prayers Together: 60 Reflections on the Anglican Collects* (London: Church Society, 2023), p. 155. See also the collects for the tenth and nineteenth Sundays after Trinity, which have a similar focus.

Something to ponder

1 Why is it difficult to think that the works of unbelievers *cannot* please God?

2 Have you submitted your life to the King, or are you still somehow in rebellion, trying to be independent? Ask for his help to lay down your arms.

3 In what ways are you tempted to be half-hearted in following Jesus? What can you do about it?

4 Praise God that he accepts even our most feeble and weak efforts to please him as believers.

4

Rejoicing in repentance

But if a wicked person turns away from all the sins they have committed and keeps all my decrees and does what is just and right, that person will surely live; they will not die. None of the offenses they have committed will be remembered against them. Because of the righteous things they have done, they will live. Do I take any pleasure in the death of the wicked? declares the Sovereign LORD. Rather, am I not pleased when they turn from their ways and live?

But if a righteous person turns from their righteousness and commits sin and does the same detestable things the wicked person does, will they live? None of the righteous things that person has done will be remembered. Because of the unfaithfulness they are guilty of and because of the sins they have committed, they will die.

Yet you say, 'The way of the Lord is not just.' Hear, you Israelites: Is my way unjust? Is it not your ways that are unjust? If a righteous person turns from their righteousness and commits sin, they will die for it; because of the sin they have committed they will die. But if a wicked person turns away from the wickedness they have committed and does what is just and right, they will save their life. Because they consider all the offenses they have committed and turn away from them, that person will surely live; they will not die. Yet the Israelites say, 'The way of the Lord is not just.' Are my ways unjust, people of Israel? Is it not your ways that are unjust?

Therefore, you Israelites, I will judge each of you according to your own ways, declares the Sovereign LORD. Repent! Turn

away from all your offenses; then sin will not be your downfall. Rid yourselves of all the offenses you have committed, and get a new heart and a new spirit. Why will you die, people of Israel? For I take no pleasure in the death of anyone, declares the Sovereign LORD. Repent and live!
(Ezekiel 18:21–32)

It was my very first RE lesson at secondary school. As an 11-year-old I had no idea what to expect of a religious education class, and I was quite surprised by the first question the teacher asked us. He said, 'What is your ambition in life? What is your purpose?'

Everyone went quiet. A few boys said, 'To be a rock star' or 'To be a millionaire'. But when his eyes settled on me I could only think of one thing. My ambition? 'To please God, sir.'

Well, I think it must have been a good answer because he immediately awarded me 10 house points like they do at Hogwarts in Harry Potter, and then rather confusingly (and worryingly) told me to stay behind after class.

As I anxiously watched the other boys leave, the teacher asked me if I meant what I said about my ambition being to please God. I mumbled an embarrassed 'yes'. He then proceeded to probe me expertly with questions about my Christian commitment. I had prayed a prayer to put Jesus Christ first in my life just a few weeks earlier, so I was relieved to be able to answer his questions. But it wasn't an inquisition; he was gently trying to help and encourage me, as a fellow believer.

The history of my teenage years wasn't exactly about giving uninterrupted pleasure to God … I didn't really understand what that meant until later. And I had only the vaguest idea of how to find out what pleases the Lord. We had a few books at home of course. One of which was *Answers to a Child: An Aid to Parents in Teaching Their Children about Religion* by Dorothy Whitcombe. I don't remember reading it back then, but I might have done.

This book is quite helpful in many respects and I was looking for answers. We shouldn't tell kids that God lives in the sky, for instance, it says. There's an amusing story here about a child who got upset at a fireworks display. As a large rocket was let off:

> a small shocked voice said, 'Oh-h-h, they shouldn't do that.' I said soothingly, 'It's alright, darling, they won't hurt anyone.' '[But] they'll hit God' I was told firmly. A minute later, when a very high one tore up into the sky, he added, 'Got Him!' with conviction.[1]

So, don't tell kids that God lives in the sky! Good advice there. But I was quite disappointed when I read this on page 13:

> Then there is the question of the Old Testament … Many may disagree but I do believe that only the New Testament should be taught until a child is old enough to understand the two utterly different conceptions of God. Surely they must learn to know God the Father before the quite different, and very often terrifying, portrayal of God in the Old Testament.
>
> Of course there are wonderful stories there, but many have far from Christian standards of right and wrong. It does seem better to leave the Old Testament for later years when it can be realised that in those days people were guessing about God.

A little later, in the chapter entitled, 'Mummy, who is God exactly?', our author urges us not to read to our children 'stories of the God of wrath and vengeance in the Old Testament'.[2] Modern atheists such as Richard Dawkins would agree of course. He says this:

---

1 Dorothy Whitcombe, *Answers to a Child: An Aid to Parents in Teaching Their Children about Religion* (London: Mowbray, 1959), p. 12.

2 Whitcombe, *Answers to a Child*, p. 20.

The God of the Old Testament is arguably the most unpleasant character in all fiction: jealous and proud of it; a petty, unjust, unforgiving control-freak; a vindictive, blood-thirsty ethnic cleanser; a misogynistic, homophobic, racist, infanticidal, genocidal, filicidal, pestilential, megalomaniacal, sadomasochistic, capriciously malevolent bully.[3]

There's a lot we could say in response to this sort of thing. But what's interesting for our purposes here is that in Dorothy Whitcombe's view, and Richard Dawkins' view, the God of the Old Testament loves to judge. He is full of wrath and anger, and enjoys smiting his enemies with bolts of lightning. Is that true?

God does not enjoy judgement

The seventeenth-century theologian John Owen once said, 'For what doth please God, God himself is the sole judge.'[4] So the best place to turn to find out what makes him happy or sad is God's word. And when we do that, we find that if we see him as a nasty God full of hate who loves to judge, we have been given a false impression. That picture of him is not what we hear about in Ezekiel 18 from the Old Testament, at the top of this chapter. Ezekiel tells us there that God does not enjoy judgement. Instead, we hear: 'Do I take any pleasure in the death of the wicked? declares the Sovereign LORD. Rather, am I not pleased when they turn from their ways and live?'

God does not enjoy judgement. He does not enjoy the death of the wicked, the pronouncing of a divine death sentence against evil. But yes, God *will* judge. He is not a soft god, a god without moral boundaries or a sense of right and wrong. Verse 30 says, 'Therefore,

---

3 Richard Dawkins, *The God Delusion* (London: Bantam Press, 2006), p. 31.

4 John Owen, *The Works of John Owen*, ed. W. H. Goold (Edinburgh: Johnstone & Hunter, 1854), 9:72.

you Israelites, I will judge each of you according to your own ways, declares the Sovereign LORD.' Yes, God will judge. But he prefers to forgive. He would be far happier, so to speak, if we abandoned our rebellion against him expressed in a lifestyle of pleasure-seeking, me-first materialism.

God would much rather we turned away from that and enjoyed life as it was meant to be lived in harmony with him. So, verse 27: 'But if a wicked person turns away from the wickedness they have committed and does what is just and right, they will save their life.' That's why he calls to the people in verse 30:

Repent! Turn away from all your offenses; then sin will not be your downfall. Rid yourselves of all the offenses you have committed, and get a new heart and a new spirit. Why will you die, people of Israel? For I take no pleasure in the death of anyone, declares the Sovereign LORD. Repent and live!

There were some people in Ezekiel's day who didn't like the idea of God forgiving wicked people. Why should they get off, just because they change their ways and turn back to God?! So we see in verse 25 they were saying, 'The way of the Lord is not just.' It's not fair for God to forgive. But they were also upset at verse 24:

But if a righteous person turns from their righteousness and commits sin and does the same detestable things the wicked person does, will they live? None of the righteous things that person has done will be remembered. Because of the unfaithfulness they are guilty of and because of the sins they have committed, they will die.

Why should people who have done good things in the past be judged for bad things they do later on in life? Surely the good can outweigh the bad? Surely we can pay our dues to God early on in life and that will count for something later on when we choose to go our own way? But no, God says he doesn't care about our history or our pedigree. He's not bothered by how committed we *used* to be, or how often we *used* to go to church. He's only interested in today, and whether we have continued to turn away from our sin. It doesn't impress God that we prayed a prayer of commitment to him when we were younger, if today we're only living for ourselves. What pleases him is when we keep turning back to him for forgiveness.

God loves repentance

If Dorothy Whitcombe is to be believed, the New Testament should give us an 'utterly different conception' of God. But is that true? Let's look at what Jesus said on the subject in this famous parable from Luke 15. As you read it, think: 'What pleases God?'

Jesus continued: 'There was a man who had two sons. The younger one said to his father, "Father, give me my share of the estate." So he divided his property between them.

'Not long after that, the younger son got together all he had, set off for a distant country and there squandered his wealth in wild living. After he had spent everything, there was a severe famine in that whole country, and he began to be in need. So he went and hired himself out to a citizen of that country, who sent him to his fields to feed pigs. He longed to fill his stomach with the pods that the pigs were eating, but no one gave him anything.

'When he came to his senses, he said, "How many of my father's hired servants have food to spare, and here I am starving to death! I will set out and go back to my father and say to him: Father, I have sinned against heaven and against you. I am no longer worthy to be called your son; make me like one of your hired servants." So he got up and went to his father.

'But while he was still a long way off, his father saw him and was filled with compassion for him; he ran to his son, threw his arms around him and kissed him.

'The son said to him, "Father, I have sinned against heaven and against you. I am no longer worthy to be called your son."

'But the father said to his servants, "Quick! Bring the best robe and put it on him. Put a ring on his finger and sandals on his feet. Bring the fattened calf and kill it. Let's have a feast and celebrate. For this son of mine was dead and is alive again; he was lost and is found." So they began to celebrate.

'Meanwhile, the older son was in the field. When he came near the house, he heard music and dancing. So he called one of the servants and asked him what was going on. "Your brother has come," he replied, "and your father has killed the fattened calf because he has him back safe and sound."

'The older brother became angry and refused to go in. So his father went out and pleaded with him. But he answered his father, "Look! All these years I've been slaving for you and never disobeyed your orders. Yet you never gave me even a young goat so I could celebrate with my friends. But when this son of yours who has squandered your property with prostitutes comes home, you kill the fattened calf for him!"

'"My son," the father said, "you are always with me, and everything I have is yours. But we had to celebrate and be glad, because this brother of yours was dead and is alive again; he was lost and is found."'

(Luke 15:11–32)

This passage from the New Testament says a lot about what makes God smile. I think I knew this story when I was 11. It's quite familiar. But I don't think I realised it contained the answer to how I could fulfil my life's ambition.

So what pleases God? When many people today think of God, they think of him either as a benevolent grandfatherly figure who smiles benignly at everything we do, or as an angry ogre in the sky who likes nothing more than to smite people for no good reason and demands adoration from servile followers. But we don't need to guess about the nature of God; God himself tells us very clearly – he is a God who loves repentance. As R. C. Sproul put it, 'Certainly this parable makes it clear that nothing is more pleasing to God than our sincere sorrowing over sin and turning from it.'[5]

All the parables in Luke 15 are basically Jesus' answer to the grumbling Pharisees and scribes at the beginning of the chapter.[6] 'Now the tax collectors and sinners were all gathering around to hear Jesus. But the Pharisees and the teachers of the law muttered, "This man welcomes sinners and eats with them"' (Luke 15:1–2). They're grumbling and complaining because Jesus associates with people they do not consider worthy, just like those in Ezekiel's day who didn't like the idea of God forgiving certain people. But Jesus spends time with and welcomes the dregs of society, the untouchables, the outcasts. He spends time with the religious leaders too – Luke shows him meeting and eating with Pharisees as well (Luke 14:1). But he didn't only associate with *them*. These people of ill repute, these less respectable people, wanted to hear Jesus too, and the Pharisees and Bible experts didn't like it. It didn't seem right to them that this great teacher and prophet should mix with such people.

To justify his policy of spending time with those who were labelled 'sinners', Jesus tells three stories, or parables. The key

---

5 R. C. Sproul, *Pleasing God: Discovering the Meaning and Importance of Sanctification*, 2nd edition (Colorado Springs, CO: David C. Cook, 2012), chapter 7.

6 How the parable particularly speaks to the scribes, the teachers of the law, is brilliantly brought out by Peter Williams, *The Surprising Genius of Jesus: What the Gospels Reveal about the Greatest Teacher* (Wheaton, IL: Crossway, 2023).

points are the same in all three: God eagerly searches for people who are lost, and he celebrates when he finds them.

We see this in the parable of the lost sheep. The shepherd loses one sheep, so he leaves the ninety-nine and goes looking for the lost one. When he finds it he is overjoyed. Jesus concludes Luke 15:7 with: 'Just so, I tell you, there will be more joy in heaven over one sinner who repents than over ninety-nine righteous persons who need no repentance' (ESV).

Joy in heaven! A party to celebrate the recovery of what was lost. It's the same point in the parable of the lost coin. The woman loses one of her coins. She looks high and low to find it. When she does, she's not only relieved; she's ecstatic. Luke 15:10: 'Just so, I tell you, there is joy before the angels of God over one sinner who repents' (ESV).

God is like the shepherd. God is like the woman. He eagerly searches for lost people – like the sinners and tax collectors – and celebrates when he finds them. He loves finding sinners. They are 'found' when they repent. That is, we know God has found them when they turn back to him. God does not enjoy judgement but rather he loves repentance – he loves finding people and saving them from being lost forever.

That's basically the message of the parable of the prodigal son too. Or rather, as it should be called, the parable of the forgiving father. Because it's the father who's the most important character in the story, not the son who runs away and squanders his father's wealth in wild living. We're meant to see the connection to the other two parables. God is the father figure who rejoices at the repentance of his wayward son coming home. And we're meant to see his connection to the sinners and tax collectors – God loves that they're crowding round to hear Jesus. It means they're thinking of coming home.

So this is the doctrine. In a sense, God does not delight in wrath and vengeance, either in the New Testament or in the Old. He will judge, because he is the moral arbiter of the universe and there really is a difference between right and wrong. But he's a reluctant judge, in one sense. Because he much prefers to forgive. He has no pleasure in the death and judgement of anyone. He loves it when we repent and turn back to him instead. Speaking of what he calls 'communion with God', John Owen said:

> It is the gladness of the heart of Christ, the joy of his soul, to take poor sinners into this relation with himself. He rejoiced in the thoughts of it from eternity, Prov. 8:31; and always expresses the greatest willingness to undergo the hard task required for that.[7]

That's why, 'for the joy set before him', Jesus 'endured the cross, scorning its shame' (Hebrews 12:2). He did it gladly, for us and for our salvation.

Come home!

So what's the application of this for us? I think there are two things. First, if you want to please God, the clear message is: come home! The pastor–theologians of the important international gathering known as the Synod of Dort (1618–19) declared with passion: 'God seriously and most truly shows in His Word what is pleasing to Him, namely that those called would come to Him.'[8]

Return to God, and he will receive you with open arms. The father in Luke 15:20 felt compassion and ran and embraced his son and kissed him. And we may feel, like the son, that we don't deserve his favour. We may not feel that we deserve his love and

---

7 Owen, *Works*, 2:55. I have updated the language slightly.

8 For the translation, see W. Robert Godfrey, *Saving the Reformation: The Pastoral Theology of the Canons of Dort* (Sanford, FL: Reformation Trust, 2019), p. 55 (Canons of Dort 3/4.8).

kindness. We may have made a complete and utter mess of our lives, whether openly or in secret; there may be shameful ways we'd rather not talk about. We may feel that we deserve nothing but God's anger and condemnation and that we could never be pleasing to him.

But God stands ready to forgive. He doesn't want to judge us. It gives him no pleasure to see us wallowing in the pigsty or languishing in hell forever. Make no mistake – he is a righteous, just and all-seeing God. Nothing will escape his gaze and all will be laid bare on his day of judgement. But he would rather we repent, turn back to him, and ask for mercy. He wants us to come home, having discovered and admitted that life without him wasn't quite the party we might have expected.

The Father calls us to come home with no worries of being rejected. If we're even considering going back; if we're even fortunate enough to hear this call today to return home, then we can be sure – he is already eagerly searching for us.

No one need fear rejection – however far away they have strayed. There should be no worries about rejection and, what's more, there's no point in delay. Can't we hear him calling in Ezekiel 18:31: 'Why will you die?' Why don't you choose life instead and come back to the source of all goodness and truth and light?

We might delay coming back for many reasons. Because we're not sure God exists, or that he's really like this. It's not wrong to ask questions and get these things straight in our heads. But if we know it's true, there's no point in delaying. Don't wait for a significant milestone in your life, or put it off until the new year. You never know how long you might have. 'Seek the LORD while he may be found; call on him while he is near' (Isaiah 55:6). He may not be near forever.

Augustine says this: 'Say not then, "Tomorrow I will turn, tomorrow I will please God; and all today's and yesterday's deeds shall be forgiven me" … God has promised pardon to your conversion; He has not promised a tomorrow to your delay.'[9] And Charles Spurgeon encourages us with this: '"Without faith it is impossible to please God," but it gives God a divine pleasure to see the first grain of mustard seed of faith in a poor, turning sinner's heart.'[10]

The Dutch author, Rutger Bregman, tells the wonderful story of how Colombia's defence minister hired an advertising agency to help in that country's struggle against a well-established guerrilla army which had been wreaking havoc in a seemingly never-ending war. With the ad agency, the Colombian military set up Operation Christmas in December 2010. They put up thousands of Christmas lights on giant trees in strategic places. When a guerrilla fighter approached to see this strange sight, motion detectors were activated which lit up a banner, reading: 'If Christmas can come to the jungle, you can come home. Demobilise. At Christmas, everything is possible.' Within a few weeks, hundreds laid down their weapons.

The next year, in Operation Rivers of Light, the families of guerrilla fighters were encouraged to write letters saying, 'Come home, we're waiting for you.' These were placed inside thousands of floating LED-illuminated balls and dropped into the rivers which the guerrilla army used to navigate around the countryside. Almost 200 more gave up their weapons. The next year, Operation Bethlehem saw thousands more lights dropped from military helicopters as beacons to show the fighters their way home, like the star of Bethlehem guiding the wise men to Jesus.

Later, the Colombian secret service obtained a list of women who had children in the guerrilla army. Some of them had not seen their

---

9 Augustine of Hippo, *Expositions on the Book of Psalms* in *Saint Augustin: Expositions on the Book of Psalms*, ed. P. Schaff, tr. A. C. Coxe (New York, NY: Christian Literature Company, 1888), 8:658 (quoting Ecclesiasticus 5:7 from the Apocrypha). I have updated the English a little.

10 C. H. Spurgeon, 'Pleading and Encouragement' in *The Metropolitan Tabernacle Pulpit Sermons* (London: Passmore & Alabaster, 1884), 30:454.

sons and daughters for many, many years. The ad agency asked them for childhood photographs of these men and women, which only they would recognise, and then spread them throughout the area where the army was fighting. On each photograph was also a caption; it read, 'Before you were a guerrilla, you were my child.' More than 200 more soon returned home to their parents, to be granted amnesty by the government and retraining in more fruitful trades.[11]

Elsewhere, the story is also told of a mother in South America. You may have heard it before. It's the story of a mother whose daughter ran away from home to live it up in the city. She quickly found that life was not always as rosy as she'd imagined. Things got rough when the money ran out, and she ended up as a prostitute.

As you can imagine, her mother couldn't bear doing nothing; yet she didn't know what to do. But eventually she decided to go into the city and look for her daughter. When she couldn't find her, she took hundreds of passport photos of herself and pinned them up in hotels and bars all over the city in the hope that her daughter would recognise her.

One day, the daughter saw one of them in a cheap hotel she happened to be in. She recognised her mother immediately and grabbed the photo. She turned it over in her hands, and there in her mother's handwriting on the back it simply said, 'Wherever you are, whatever you've done, come home.'

The mother was undoubtedly grieved at the daughter turning her back on her. And grieved by what she'd then done with her life. But whatever she thought about her daughter, she hadn't for one moment stopped loving her and wanting her back.

It's just the same with God. He's grieved by our sin, our ongoing guerrilla warfare against him, but not for a moment has he stopped loving us, and wanting us to come back. He longs for us to return,

---

11 Rutger Bregman, *Humankind: A Hopeful History,* tr. Elizabeth Manton and Erica Moore (London: Bloomsbury, 2020), chapter 18.

demobilise, lay down our arms, and follow the light that came into the world at Bethlehem during the first Operation Christmas. Millions of Christians have been left in this world as beacons, as images of Christ, to arrest our attention and direct us to his message of forgiveness, amnesty and a more fruitful life.

So why delay? Why put it off any longer? If we've got a home to go to, and a father who loves us – why wait?

You might be thinking: 'But God won't accept *me*. I'm not as respectable as these other people I know who go to church. God wouldn't want me …'

Wherever you are, whatever you've done – come home.

'God won't accept me. I'm not the religious type. I didn't even know that Ezekiel was in the Old Testament, and I only ever say "Jesus" when I'm swearing …'

Wherever you are, whatever you've done – come home.

'God won't accept me. I've been here so many times before. I just keep on failing him, letting him down again and again. He must surely have run out of patience with me, and there can't be any other addicts or adulterers or angry ill-disciplined people like me among his people …'

Wherever you are, whatever you've done – come home.

God has no pleasure in judgement, even though as the moral arbiter of the universe he *must* judge. He loves repentance, and goes looking for sinners. As John Piper puts it, 'Who can comprehend that God continually burns with hot anger at the rebellion of the wicked and grieves over the unholy speech of his people (Ephesians 4:29–30), yet takes pleasure in them daily (Psalm 149:4), and ceaselessly makes merry over penitent prodigals who come home?'[12] So come home. Or if you can't manage that, at least pray that God would give you the ability to repent. Spurgeon assures us:

---

12 John Piper, *The Pleasures of God* (Fearn, Ross-shire: Mentor, 2001), p. 72.

Ay, let me say it joyfully, the saving works of Jesus are lovely in the Father's eyes. Whenever our Lord Jesus says to a sinner, 'I absolve you,' it pleases God; whenever the Saviour calls a wanderer to himself and draws him to holiness by the attractions of his love it pleases God ... It is the pleasure of God that sinners should find a complete Saviour in Jesus. The Father has no pleasure in the death of the wicked, but had rather that he should turn unto him and live, but there is joy in the heart of God himself over sinners that repent ... Prodigals leaving their riotous living are pressed to the Father's bosom and cause pleasure to the soul of the benign Deity. Oh, returning sinners, you have not to ask Christ to appease the Father, for the Father himself loves you, and your salvation gives him joy.[13]

Rejoice with him

Finally, there's something else we should notice about these parables Jesus told. They are not just teaching us about God's love of our repentance. They are inviting us *to share it.* They are inviting us to rejoice with God.

Have a look at a curious detail which is often missed in the first two parables in Luke 15. The shepherd finds his sheep and then rejoices. Is that what it says? Yes, but that's not all. Luke 15 verse 6: 'Then he calls his friends and neighbors together and says, "*Rejoice with me*; I have found my lost sheep"' (emphasis added).

And then again in the second parable. The woman finds her coin, and she is glad. So then, verse 9, 'when she finds it, she calls her friends and neighbors together and says, "*Rejoice with me*; I have found my lost coin"' (emphasis added).

It seems a strange and unnecessary detail if the only message is that God loves repentance. In both cases there's something more.

---

13 Spurgeon, 'The Christian's Motto' in *The Metropolitan Tabernacle Pulpit Sermons*, 20:184. I have updated the language slightly.

The figure that stands for God – the shepherd or the woman – invites friends and neighbours to join in their rejoicing. Because God's friends share God's delight in the recovery of the lost.

The parable of the forgiving father is no different. The father has two sons. His second son is unhappy with the lavish welcome given to his wayward brother. Clearly, if the prodigal son is a picture of the sinners and tax collectors flocking to hear Jesus, then this elder son is meant to be the Pharisees and scribes themselves. They've been grumbling about Jesus' warm welcome for those less respectable, less pious, than themselves. Like the elder brother, they hear that God has received such people, and they are angry and refuse to join the party. They don't love repentance. They love the status quo. They have a passion for devout respectability. They're quite happy to be the only ones (seemingly) enjoying privileged access to the father, and they don't really want to share it. Jesus pictures God the Father coming out to plead with these Pharisaical older brothers. God implores them to be happy that the prodigal has come home, and that sinners are turning back to God. But they're not. They resent the extravagant attention being given to the newcomers. They grumble and complain because the father is so gracious and kind.

There are always two choices when we're confronted with God's grace. We can either join him in the party, rejoice in his generosity to those who don't deserve it, and go looking for other lost sheep whose recovery will gladden the heart of God. Or we can grumble: 'This church is for people like *us*, not them. We don't want them dragging our good reputation down.' Would we rather celebrate with our friends while our brothers rot in the pigsty – as they deserve – or will we be as compassionate as the father, and celebrate with him when our brothers come home?

It feels like a very unsatisfactory ending to the story because we don't know what the elder brother did. Did he swallow his pride, smile with his father and make up with his brother? Or did he stomp off in a huff? The reason Jesus doesn't tell us the ending is because he's inviting the Pharisees, and he's inviting us, to write the ending ourselves. He's inviting us to join the party and serve God by reaching out to those who are far off. Are we God's friends who share in his delight in the recovery of the lost?

As the medieval gospel preacher John Wycliffe (1330–84) said, 'If you wish to please God, you ought [to] detest pride in your thinking, in your mind, and in your life ... the more humble a man is, the swifter he is in God's service.'[14] So will we, like the shepherd, go looking for the sheep?

There may be many bad motives for inviting friends to hear a gospel talk. For example, it might feel as though it will be great for our reputation in the church if we fill a whole table at an evangelistic event with our non-Christian friends. Perhaps we covet the awe of our Bible-study group who say, 'Wow, what a great evangelist!' But there are many good motives for being involved in evangelism: love for our friends – we don't want to see them lost and without Jesus, destined to spend eternity separated from him. We don't want to see them waste their lives without the purpose and forgiveness, and the strength, that he brings. And we know we have an obligation to them too: we have the good news of salvation – we know that there's a cure for sin, an antidote to its poison, and a way of escape on judgement day. How can we not share that with others? How can we keep it all for ourselves?

Yet the highest motive to drive any Christian, as we've seen throughout this book, is the desire to please God and be enjoyed by him. And what more proof do we need that being involved in the plan to rescue the lost is pleasing to God than the words of Jesus himself: there is joy in heaven over one sinner who repents. As Spurgeon preached:

'Well, what could I do that would please God?' you say. First, I should think you could look for his lost children. That is

14 John Wycliffe, *Trialogus*, tr. Stephen E. Lahey (Cambridge: Cambridge University Press, 2013), p. 141 (III.11).

sure to please him. Go tonight, and see whether you cannot find one of the erring whom you might bring back to the fold. Would you not please a mother, if she had lost her baby, and you set to work to find it? We want to please God. Seek the lost ones, and bring them in.[15]

So let's not think that just because our unbelieving friends might struggle with their temper or their sexuality or their honesty or their faithfulness that they are beyond the pale. Wherever they are, whatever they've done, God longs for them to come home. The church of Jesus Christ is a fellowship of sinners, a rough and ragged bunch, not a cosy club for the smug and self-righteous. If God does not enjoy judgement but prefers to see people repent and live, then that too should be our creed, and our delight.

Prayer

Heavenly Father,
you delight in showing mercy,
and sent your Son to save us and bring us home.
Give us grace to repent of our sins
and turn to Christ in faith,
that we may bring joy to your heart
and a new passion to our lives
in the perfect freedom of serving Jesus.
Amen.

Something to ponder

1 Do you sometimes secretly suspect that the God of the Old Testament is different from the God of the New? How can you talk to yourself about that?

---

15 Spurgeon, 'Praise for the Gift of Gifts' in *The Metropolitan Tabernacle Pulpit Sermons*, 38:131.

2 If God loves repentance, what's stopping you coming home to him?

3 If God's friends share God's delight in the recovery of the lost, how is this visible in your life?

4 Praise God that he is a kind and forgiving Father, who sent his Son to save us and his Spirit to change us.

5

Delightful worship

Then Noah built an altar to the LORD and, taking some of all the clean animals and clean birds, he sacrificed burnt offerings on it. The Lord smelled the pleasing aroma and said in his heart: 'Never again will I curse the ground because of humans, even though every inclination of the human heart is evil from childhood.'
(Genesis 8:20–1)

The old Puritan preacher Thomas Manton declares: 'The main intent of the soul must be to please God, as his will must be the rule of your life; so his glory must be the end of your lives.'[1] Yet how many of us live to please ourselves and bring glory to ourselves? For a Christian, however, our joy is intimately linked to God's joy; as Spurgeon once said, 'The greatest joy of a Christian is to give joy to Christ.'[2]

What is it then that brings Christ joy? What does he like and dislike? What pleases him? If you gather up all the references to pleasing God in the Bible and categorise them, it's easy to spot a big group of them which refer to what we might call 'worship'. That is, they have something to do with religious ceremonies, particularly the Old Testament sacrificial system, and God's religious requirements.

---

1 Thomas Manton, *The Complete Works of Thomas Manton* (London: James Nisbet & Co., 1872), 14:59.

2 C. H. Spurgeon, 'My Garden – His Garden' in *The Metropolitan Tabernacle Pulpit Sermons* (London: Passmore & Alabaster, 1896), 42:356.

A relaxing fragrance

Much of the language in these verses about pleasing God is related to earthly things like food, drink and smell, as in the passage above. Noah sacrificed burnt offerings to the Lord after the Flood, and 'the LORD smelled the pleasing aroma and said in his heart: "Never again will I curse the ground because of humans, even though every inclination of the human heart is evil from childhood"'. The first thing Noah does after he and the animals come out of the ark is to offer a sacrifice to God by way of thanksgiving. And did you notice how it is described? God smelled the *pleasing aroma*. Literally, the phrase there is, 'he smelled the soothing scent'. That is, the smell was quieting, pleasant and calming. It conjures up the picture of a nice warm bath, full of aromatherapy oils. It's a comforting, relaxing fragrance. And this becomes a standard phrase in the Bible to mean something that is pleasing to God. (Actually, in Hebrew the word is also related to Noah's name, which means comfort.)

In Leviticus 1 we read about how to perform the ritual sacrifices and offerings of bulls and goats and sheep. And the phrase comes many times: it is a pleasing aroma to the Lord. God likes the smell of roast beef and roast lamb. And in Numbers 15 we hear that he also likes the smell of fine wine. And there are grain offerings and fresh warm bread offerings too.

In other ancient cultures there was this idea that the gods smell a sacrifice and then crowd like flies around it because they're hungry. But the biblical idea is not quite like that. The idea is *not* that God's hunger is satisfied by this food. So God says in Psalm 50:12–13, 'If I were hungry, I would not tell you, for the world and its fullness are mine. Do I eat the flesh of bulls or drink the blood of goats?' (ESV). In other words, I don't need your sacrifices because I'm hungry. I own the cattle on a thousand hills, so if it was just meat I wanted then I've got more than enough.

No, God doesn't need our offerings. The biblical idea behind these pleasing sacrifices is that because the sacrifice is offered by faith, God's anger is put to rest. That's what caused the Flood in Noah's day, after all – God's righteous anger and judgement against human rebellion. Noah was saved by faith; he was spared from the deluge because he trusted God's word of warning. As Hebrews 11:7 says, 'By faith Noah, when warned about things not yet seen, in holy fear built an ark to save his family.' So God's anger is pacified, propitiated if you like, by the smell of the sacrifice, a sacrifice which symbolises a wholehearted and faithful commitment to him. The key point is that he is pleased by the heart of faith that lies behind the performance of the so-called religious act.

A foul stench

Sometimes, however, our worship does not smell so good. This is emphasised in the stinging rebuke which the prophet Malachi delivers to God's people at the end of the Old Testament. The problem in Malachi is that God's people doubt that God still cares for them. And this doubt expresses itself in various aspects of their relationship to God. In Malachi 1 the issue is the sacrificial system in the Temple at Jerusalem. God tells the people that they don't respect or honour him any more. They in response query this, to which God, through Malachi, replies that they are offering second-rate – lame or diseased – animals for sacrifice (Malachi 1:6–8).

Why are they doing this? It's because they think that if God doesn't care about them any more, why should they care about him? They come to the Temple thinking, 'Let's just get it all over and done with, perform our spiritual duties, and then get out of there.' The attitude of wanting to glorify and please God in what they do is missing. So God says, 'When you offer blind animals for sacrifice, is that not wrong? When you sacrifice lame or diseased animals, is that not wrong? Try offering them to your governor! Would he be pleased with you? Would he accept you?' (Malachi 1:8).

Would a secular ruler be happy with such slapdash, inferior offerings? Would it secure you a bigger bonus during your end-of-year review if you behaved in such a way towards your boss? I think not. So Malachi 1:10 says, 'Oh, that one of you would shut the temple doors, so that you would not light useless fires on my altar! I am not pleased with you ... and I will accept no offering from your hands.' God does not want their shoddy sacrifices, and has no pleasure in them. God would rather close the Temple and shut everything down than carry on with the charade of careless, half-hearted worship.

God doesn't *need* us. His happiness does not hinge on us doing 'the religion thing'. As John Piper puts it:

> We need to see first and foremost that God is overflowingly happy in the eternal fellowship of the Trinity, and that he does not need us to complete his fullness and is not deficient without us. Rather *we* are deficient without *him*; the all-sufficient glory of God, freely given in fellowship through his sacrificed Son, is the stream of living water that we have thirsted for all our lives.[3]

But clearly there was a problem in Malachi's day. It's not that the people then were not performing their religious duties, because they were. Nominally they were doing exactly what they should. But their hearts weren't in it. They thirsted for something else other than God, and that showed in their worship.

Sadly we see this theme throughout the Old Testament. So Isaiah 1:11 says:

---

3 John Piper, *The Pleasures of God* (Fearn, Ross-shire: Mentor, 2001), p. 22.

> 'The multitude of your sacrifices –
>> what are they to me?' says the LORD.
> 'I have more than enough of burnt offerings,
>> of rams and the fat of fattened animals;
> I have no pleasure
>> in the blood of bulls and lambs and goats.'

That is, God used to delight in the worship he had appointed for them to use. But he does so no longer, not now that their hearts are far away. In Amos 5:21–3, God speaks similarly of their meetings and songs:

> I hate, I despise your religious festivals;
>> your assemblies are a stench to me.
> Even though you bring me burnt offerings and grain
>> offerings,
> I will not accept them.
> Though you bring choice fellowship offerings,
>> I will have no regard for them.
> Away with the noise of your songs!
>> I will not listen to the music of your harps.

What has gone wrong? Again, it's not that they aren't 'doing the religious thing'. They do it very well – to human eyes. Even the music and singing. They are a very religious people, but they've forgotten the more important things: trust in God, and faithful discipleship. As Thomas Manton says, 'A renewed heart, that is unfeignedly set to please God in all things, is more than all the pomp of external duties.'[4] You can see that clearly if you look more at the contexts of Isaiah 1 and Amos 5. So the great prophet and judge, Samuel, sums it up well, saying in 1 Samuel 15:22: 'Does the

---

4 Manton, *Complete Works*, 2:15.

Lord delight in burnt offerings and sacrifices as much as in obeying the Lord? To obey is better than sacrifice, and to heed is better than the fat of rams.'

This is a key text for understanding what pleases God. God delights in sacrifices – yes, when they are performed by faith, out of a heart that loves and trusts and relies on God completely. Those smell good. But even the most costly sacrifices don't please God when things like justice, mercy and obedience are ignored.

Samuel said those devastating words to King Saul. And the next verse was the end of his reign, effectively, as God rejected him as king. The man who replaced him had a much better idea of what pleases God. King David knew the relative importance of sacrifices and obedience. So that even when he failed most spectacularly, by sleeping with a married woman and then arranging for her husband to die in battle, he knew what he had to do.

Psalm 51 is his prayer after that terrible incident. In this psalm, David prays to God and confesses not just to adultery and murder but to being full of sin, transgression and iniquity. He wonders what he can do in return for God's gracious forgiveness of him. He prays, in verse 16, 'You do not delight in sacrifice, or I would bring it; you do not take pleasure in burnt offerings.' In other words, he knows he can't palm God off with a few sacrifices of sheep or goats or bulls. Technically they might give off 'pleasing aromas'; but to God they would be a rotten stench. So David says in verse 17, 'My sacrifice, O God, is a broken spirit; a broken and contrite heart you, God, will not despise.'

To obey is better than sacrifice, said Samuel. To repent and mean it is what really counts, says David. That's what truly brings a smile to God's face again. But then, he concludes in Psalm 51:18–19, 'May it please you to prosper Zion, to build up the walls of Jerusalem. Then you will delight in the sacrifices of the righteous, in burnt offerings offered whole; then bulls will be offered on your altar.' So

God can still *delight* in right sacrifices. But only in the context of a broken spirit and a contrite heart.

The right aroma

So what have we seen so far? We've seen that the sacrificial system pleases God when it is operated as intended by people of faith – that is, when the offerings are made with a sense of gratitude, dependence and love for God. In that case, the smell of sacrificed animals is a pleasing aroma, soothing his anger against sin.

But if the sacrifices are given without that right attitude and disposition, even a 'pleasing aroma' is a foul stench to God. To use a human analogy: if a husband and wife fall out or have a blazing row, it can't be patched up by one or other of them going upstairs to spray on a bit of perfume, or aftershave. Normally such things would be pleasant and attractive to the other, but without that right relationship the scent means nothing. A nice smell is no replacement for a good relationship.

But so often we try this trick with God – splashing on the religious performance, spraying on a bit of piety, as if he would be impressed, as if he should be pleased we've made the effort. But he's not. That's the story of God's dealings with his people in the Old Testament: great disappointment, nominal religion and little understanding.

But Malachi, who highlights the unpleasantness of such nominal sacrifices to God, also prophesies a transformation. When the Messiah comes, he says in Malachi 3:4, he will purify people, and 'the offerings of Judah and Jerusalem will be acceptable [literally, *sweet*] to the LORD, as in days gone by, as in former years'. And so we come to my final point in this chapter. We come to the Messiah, who makes all the difference. Because Jesus has the right aroma.

Jesus Christ, the Son of God, smells great! Everything he did was pleasing to his Father. In the New Testament we see how delighted the Father is with his Son, using this very language of Old Testament worship. So in Ephesians 5:1–2, the apostle Paul says: 'Follow God's example, therefore, as dearly loved children and walk in the way of love, just as Christ loved us and gave himself up for us as a fragrant offering and sacrifice to God.' Christ loved us and gave himself up for us as 'a fragrant offering and sacrifice'. Underlying that is the same phrase we looked at earlier – 'a pleasing aroma'. It's the same Greek phrase which translates the common Old Testament idea of the sacrifices being pleasant, relaxing fragrances to God, which bring his anger to rest.

Christ offered himself up as just such a sacrifice to God. His one perfect offering of himself did away with that sacrificial system once-and-for-all. And we're told here to imitate him. Not, of course, by dying on a cross for the sins of the world. We can't do that. But by giving ourselves up in the same way; living a life of love which is pleasing to God. So when Ephesians 5:10 tells us to discern what is pleasing to the Lord, we already know what is pleasing to him – because Christ has shown the way in his own life.

We see this same truth in Hebrews 10. The writer says in verse 4 that the old sacrificial system could never properly take away our sin, but

when Christ came into the world, he said:

'Sacrifice and offering you did not desire,
    but a body you prepared for me;
with burnt offerings and sin offerings
    you were not pleased …
"I have come to do your will, my God."'

The bushy-bearded American theologian B. B. Warfield (1851–1921) sums this up well when he says, 'The purpose of the incarnation is therefore primarily to please God the Father, and to perform His will.[5] Jesus came into the world to please God.

Hebrews 10 goes on to explain that because of Christ doing the will of God, 'we have been made holy through the sacrifice of the body of Jesus Christ once for all' (verse 10). As often with Hebrews, it's a slightly complicated argument. But what the writer is saying is this: when Christ came into the world it was to fulfil Psalm 40, which is where the quotation in verses 5–7 is from. He came to replace the sacrifices and offerings, which God ultimately took no pleasure in because they were imperfect. He replaced those inadequate sacrifices with his own perfect will. That is, an obedient, holy, perfect and pleasing life. After all, it was that which God desired all along, not just the ritualistic performance of sacrifices. An obedient will is better than sacrifice.

So Christ comes to offer himself as the perfect sacrifice, in our place on the cross. He lived a perfect, sweet-smelling, God-pleasing life – and poured it out for the sake of stinking, rotten sinners.

How do you smell?

But that brings us to a final question. How do you smell? I'm not dropping hints about body odour! What I mean is: how do we smell to God? Do we smell like Jesus? That is, can we as Christians offer sacrifices which are pleasing to God? Obviously, we don't need to offer animals to God to atone for our sin or anything like that. Jesus' once-and-for-all offering of himself is utterly sufficient. In his mercy God has provided that perfect sacrifice for us. But the Bible still appeals to us, in view of God's mercy, to offer something. That's what Romans 12:1–2 says:

---

5 B. B. Warfield, *The Saviour of the World* (Edinburgh: Banner of Truth, 1991), p. 225.

> Therefore, I urge you, brothers and sisters, in view of God's mercy, to offer your bodies as a living sacrifice, holy and *pleasing to God* – this is your true and proper worship. Do not conform to the pattern of this world, but be transformed by the renewing of your mind. Then you will be able to test and approve what God's will is – his good, *pleasing* and perfect will. (emphasis added)

So, we offer our bodies, ourselves, as living sacrifices to God. Not as lambs to be slaughtered or as suicidal martyrs to seek death, but as those with renewed minds, we seek to be changed from those who follow the ways of this world to those who live to please God in everything. This is not a one-off or a once-a-week affair, but an ongoing daily act of worship, which God delights in. Just as Malachi prophesied, we have been purified to offer sacrifices which are pleasing to the Lord. So, as Charles Simeon said, 'It is not an occasional act of zeal that will please God, but a steady conscientious, uniform discharge of our duty.'[6] As Manton says, 'Our whole life should be a constant hymn to God, or a perpetual act of praise and thanksgiving.'[7]

Hebrews 13 puts a little more flesh on those bones. Christ has offered the perfect sacrifice, it says, but (Hebrews 13:15–16):

> Through Jesus, therefore, let us continually offer to God a sacrifice of praise – the fruit of lips that openly profess his name. And do not forget to do good and to share with others, for with such sacrifices God is pleased.

This is how we can smell like Jesus. We praise God continually, acknowledging his name and bringing honour to it in everything.

---

6 Charles Simeon, *Horae Homileticae: Luke XVII to John XII* (London: Holdsworth and Ball, 1833), p. 308.

7 Manton, *Complete Works*, 19:200.

And we keep doing what Jesus would do, for God is always pleased with such faith in action.

So the challenge as we look at this selection of passages on the subject of pleasing God in worship is this: do we smell of Jesus? And does God find our worship, our lives, a delight? Or are we simply going through the motions without engaging our hearts? Are we neglecting to put our faith into practice at all? In which case, we force God to hold his nose in disgust.

Prayer

O Lord and heavenly Father,
we your humble servants entirely desire your fatherly goodness
mercifully to accept our sacrifice of praise and thanksgiving;
and we most humbly ask you to grant
that by the merits and death of your Son Jesus Christ,
and through faith in his blood,
we and all your church may obtain forgiveness of our sins
and all other benefits of his death in our place.
And here we offer and present to you, O Lord,
ourselves, our souls and bodies, to be a holy and living sacrifice to
　　you.
And although we are unworthy, through our many sins,
to offer to you any sacrifice,
yet we ask you to accept our service,
not weighing our merits but pardoning our offences,
through Jesus Christ our Lord.
Amen.[8]

Something to ponder

1　Are you more concerned about the joy you get out of worshipping God than whether or not he is pleased with it?

8　This, in updated language, is the prayer after Communion from the Book of Common Prayer (1662).

2 Is there anything slapdash and half-hearted about your
   worship of God which needs addressing?
3 In what ways might you have prioritised outward performance
   over inward obedience to God in your Christian life?
4 Praise God for Jesus, whose perfect sacrifice paid the price for
   our sin and makes us acceptable to God.

6

A life of pleasure

Through Jesus, therefore, let us continually offer to God a
sacrifice of praise – the fruit of lips that openly profess his
name. And do not forget to do good and to share with others,
for with such sacrifices God is pleased.
(Hebrews 13:15–16)

A few years ago, Richard Layard, a leading economist at the
London School of Economics, published a book called *Happiness:
Lessons from a New Science*. It calls for a shift in public policy,
so that we, as a society, no longer aim for improved economic
performance and higher incomes. Instead, he wants us to
treat our feelings as paramount, and specifically for us to aim
for happiness – which, he shows, is not directly related to
income. Layard's work has been influential in some government
circles.

What's interesting is how this view clashes with what we're
looking at in this book. We've been studying the biblical theme
of living to please God. And we've discovered that our aim in life
should be to glorify God and be enjoyed by him. Lord Layard on
the other hand says this:

In the West we have a society that is probably as happy
as any there has ever been. But as we have seen, there is a
danger that me-first may pollute our way of life, now that
divine punishment no longer provides a general sanction for
morality. If that happens, we shall all be less happy. So we
do need a clear philosophy. The obvious aim is the greatest

happiness of all. If we all really pursued that, we should all be less selfish, and we should also be happier.

Through the use of reason, he says, 'we come to value the happiness of everyone equally. That should be the rule for private behaviour and for public choice. We shall not always do what is right, but if everyone tries to, we shall end up happier.'[1]

Lord Layard has great evangelistic zeal for this new alternative gospel. He gives us a new aim in life, the good news of how we can all be happier, and a vision of the end times where we all live in a happy society, having been miraculously transformed out of our 'me-first' ways of thinking. He obviously considers Christianity to have been useful in the past. It provided a threat of divine punishment to motivate people to be nice to one another and live good lives. But that no longer works, or is no longer desirable. So fear of hell needs to be replaced by a new, more positive motivation.

In his novel *Brave New World* (1932), Aldous Huxley had a similar but more frightening vision of the future. In his dystopia, happiness was also prioritised, but at the expense of truth and beauty. It was a mindless, godless place full of cookie-cutter clones, heavily controlled by brainwashing, promiscuous sex and escapist drugs, without nobility, heroism, self-control or poetry. Here the drug 'Soma' provided what Huxley called 'Christianity without tears' – virtue and perseverance and patience easily attained by taking a pill that helps you forget, in one long, mindless holiday.

I suppose what Layard and Huxley say seems in some ways a great improvement on naked capitalism where we all just accumulate as much as we can and look after number one. But we can immediately see that they appear to have misunderstood what the Bible is all about. The Bible is not about morality driven by the threat of judgement. It's about being saved from God's judgement on our

---

1 Richard Layard, *Happiness: Lessons from a New Science* (London: Allen Lane, 2005), p. 125.

self-confessed inability to do what is right. And it isn't simply about inculcating virtue and perseverance in people, via a pill or with tears. Christians don't live in fear of divine sanctions, but in thankfulness that they have been removed. We live not to escape into private pleasures, but to please the one who saved us from God's wrath which comes on those who are disobedient (Ephesians 5:6). That may well lead to us valuing the happiness of others – not because we make some rational calculation that this will create a happier society, but because this is what our saviour himself did, emptying himself and dying for us on the cross. So we imitate Jesus, to please and glorify him.

It's this wonderfully positive motivation for living that we're looking at in this chapter. If there's one text which sums up the teaching of the Bible on this subject, Hebrews 13 might well be it. Hebrews 13:16 says, 'Do not forget to do good and to share with others, for with such sacrifices God is pleased.' Doing good and sharing with others brings a smile to God's face. It's about pleasing him, not escaping his wrath. It's about delighting him, not trying to make everybody else happy.

The Bible says a lot more about what doing good and sharing with others means. And we're going to look at that now. Sometimes there is an argument between those who focus on social ethics and those who emphasise personal morality. Yet it turns out as we study the evidence that the Bible is interested in both; in our society *and* our morality. So we're going to look at how to please the one who created us, both publicly and privately. And, paradoxically perhaps, this in actual fact turns out to be for our greater good and happiness too.

Pleasing God publicly

The prophets of the Old Testament have much to say on the subject of pleasing God in our public life. Representative of their general approach is Micah 6:7–8:

Will the LORD be pleased with thousands of rams,
    with ten thousand rivers of olive oil?
Shall I offer my firstborn for my transgression,
    the fruit of my body for the sin of my soul?
He has told you, O mortal, what is good.
    And what does the LORD require of you?
To act justly and to love mercy
    and to walk humbly with your God.

The idea is that God is not pleased with thousands of animal sacrifices as much as he is with justice, kindness and humility. That word 'mercy' here can also be translated 'kindness', or 'steadfast love'. In the context, we're not talking about romantic, gooey love, but integrity. For example, a few verses later God says:

Shall I acquit someone with dishonest scales,
    with a bag of false weights?
Your rich people are violent;
    your inhabitants are liars
    and their tongues speak deceitfully.
(Micah 6:11–12)

Speaking on this text, Charles Simeon says: 'It is in vain to think that we can ever please God, if we be not honest and just in all our dealings.'[2]

In Amos 5:21–4, God doesn't tell us what pleases him, but what he *hates*. He says to a disobedient people:

I hate, I despise your religious festivals;
    your assemblies are a stench to me …
Away with the noise of your songs!

---

2   Charles Simeon, *Horae Homileticae: Hosea to Malachi* (London: Holdsworth and Bakk, 1832), p. 324.

> I will not listen to the music of your harps.
> But let justice roll on like a river,
>> righteousness like a never-failing stream!

Again, we see the emphasis on justice and righteousness being more pleasing to God than religious conformity. And this is a general theme in the prophets. Isaiah says:

> So justice is driven back,
>> and righteousness stands at a distance;
> truth has stumbled in the streets,
>> honesty cannot enter.
> Truth is nowhere to be found,
>> and whoever shuns evil becomes a prey.
>
> The LORD looked and was displeased
>> that there was no justice.
> (Isaiah 59:14–15)

Jeremiah similarly prophesies:

> 'but let the one who boasts boast about this:
>> that they have the understanding to know me,
> that I am the LORD, who exercises kindness,
>> justice and righteousness on earth,
>> *for in these I delight,'*
>>> declares the LORD.
> (Jeremiah 9:24, emphasis added)

So, from this quick look at the prophets, we get the idea that God is pleased with steadfast love, justice and righteousness. Now these are big words in the Old Testament. They are loaded with theological significance. In the context of all those texts, we see that the justice being talked about is social and economic justice in the public arena. In Amos, for instance, we hear that the people

> sell the innocent for silver,
>   and the needy for a pair of sandals.
> They trample on the heads of the poor
>   as on the dust of the ground
> (Amos 2:6–7)

In Micah it is no different: the rich oppress the poor, coveting and stealing their lands. Bribery and corruption abound, while those in charge get drunk and lord it over the others. All this is mixed in with a good dose of idolatry and heresy too. But God is just as displeased with the lack of justice. 'Justice' here means not just correct judicial decisions in courts, but fairness in all our public dealings. 'Righteousness' means correct moral and ethical standards of behaviour, not just in religious terms as we might think, but in social and economic terms as well. The word translated 'steadfast love', or 'mercy', or 'kindness', is about acting rightly, keeping vows and agreements, showing loyalty and trustworthiness. So a society where these three things – justice, righteousness and steadfast love – are lacking is neither a pleasant place to live nor a pleasant sight for God.

The book of Proverbs has much to say on this subject. Proverbs 6:16–19 teaches us that:

> There are six things the LORD hates,
>   seven that are detestable to him:
>   haughty eyes,
>   a lying tongue,
>   hands that shed innocent blood,
>   a heart that devises wicked schemes,
>   feet that are quick to rush into evil,

      a false witness who pours out lies
      and a person who stirs up conflict in the community.

Every part of the body can displease God: eyes, tongue, hands, heart. Even the smallest actions of our smallest body parts can make God feel sick. That word 'detestable' (in some versions, 'an abomination') means something God loathes or dislikes, something he find repulsive. It's the very opposite of what pleases him. And as Charles Spurgeon says, 'In pleasing God there is implied an avoiding of all things which would displease him. We cannot say we "do always the things which please him" unless we earnestly renounce the follies which vex his Holy Spirit.'[3]

We see that in verses like Proverbs 11:1 which can be seen above Greenwich Market in London: 'A false balance is [an] abomination to the LORD: but a just weight is his delight' (KJV). There's a big emphasis in other places too on this issue of false weights. It's a commercial picture of a merchant who doesn't give goods or services worth the price they're charging. So, it's a petrol station which charges a penny a litre more than it needs to, deliberately inaccurate supermarket scales, a medicine bottle that claims too much, or an estate agent who forgets to mention the rising damp and the risk of flooding. The lawyer who adds a few pounds to the hourly rate without adding any strength to the client's case. The teacher who doesn't bother to mark the coursework carefully.

Conning people upsets God. In fact, God hates all dishonesty. Just glance at Proverbs 11:20, which says, 'The LORD detests those whose hearts are perverse, but he delights in those whose ways are blameless.' Or ponder Proverbs 12:22 which tells us, 'The LORD detests lying lips, but he delights in people who are trustworthy.' The word 'delight' is contrasted again with 'detest', something God abhors and is disgusted with. God smiles when we're diligent to fill

---

3   C. H. Spurgeon, 'The Christian's Motto' in *The Metropolitan Tabernacle Pulpit Sermons* (London: Passmore & Alabaster, 1874), 20:186.

in our tax returns, insurance claims and expenses forms accurately. But he finds every lie to save a few pence nauseating. Every pound of ill-gotten gain is repugnant to him. Martin Luther says, 'You should always be more pleased with a penny and God's approval than with a whole city full of guldens [gold coins] and his abomination.'[4]

So in the public square, the prophets tell us that God delights in the big things: justice, righteousness and steadfast love. And in our dealings with others, Proverbs reminds us that God delights in fairness, accuracy and honesty. The moment we walk out of the door each day, every decision, every interaction is an opportunity – either to honour God, or to indulge in what he considers loathsome.

So this is slightly different from what Richard Layard is suggesting will make us all happy. He wants us to focus on happiness and to maximise happiness for everyone. The Bible on the other hand tells us to focus on making God happy. Do good and share with others, for this pleases *God*. Although, if society really was run along the lines suggested by the prophets and by Proverbs, there *would* be more trust, more fairness and less crime. All things which, according to Layard, make for a happy society.

The only problem is, we can't do it. As he says himself, 'We shall not always do what is right.' Economics has no answer for that and gives no real explanation of why we fail. Logic dictates that everything would be better if only we cooperated and lived this way. And that's where we often end up when we look at the Old Testament. We end up saying: this would be great, if only we could do it.

Only one person could ever say that they always did the things that were pleasing to God, and that person was Jesus, the light of the world (John 8:29).

---

4 Martin Luther, *Luther's Works*, ed. J. J. Pelikan, H. C. Oswald and H. T. Lehmann (St Louis, MO: Concordia, 1999), 51:158.

Pleasing God privately

The most amazing thing is that Jesus was not only pleasing to God in his public dealings – in religion, in business as a carpenter, and as a teacher. He was also pleasing to God in what we call the private sphere as well.

Now that's a somewhat artificial distinction – to separate public from private. To God, everything is public because he sees and knows all. Nothing is hidden from his searching gaze. And I suppose modern life has collapsed the public–private distinction too in some ways. Many people 'live online', telling everyone publicly on social media about the most intimate details of their lives. Many don't seem to have a 'private' life at all! Very much ahead of his time, the French philosopher Blaise Pascal (1623–62) seems to sum up some people's approach to social media very well:

We are not satisfied with the life we have in ourselves and our own being. We want to lead an imaginary life in the eyes of others, and so we try to make an impression. We strive constantly to embellish and preserve our imaginary being, and neglect the real one. And if we are calm or generous or loyal, we are anxious to have it known so that we can attach these virtues to our other existence.[5]

Jesus said, 'Be careful not to practice your righteousness in front of others to be seen by them. If you do, you will have no reward from your Father in heaven' (Matthew 6:1). God likes it when the public and private aspects of our lives match up. And he prefers it if we please him simply to please him, so to speak, rather than pretending to please him only to delight our 'followers' and earn their applause.

5   From Pascal's *Pensées*, no. 806. See Blaise Pascal, *Human Happiness*, tr. A. J. Krailsheimer (London: Penguin, 2008), p. 103.

There is certainly no hint in the Bible of the modern distinction often made by politicians that what they do in private has no bearing on their public life. But the Bible is clear that what we do in private is not only vitally important; it's also an indicator of how we will behave in public.

In your heart

So God is interested in our private personal morality. The Bible says we are to please God in the heart as well as with the words that we speak. As the psalmist prays, 'May these words of my mouth and this meditation of my heart be pleasing in your sight, LORD, my Rock and my Redeemer' (Psalm 19:14). The idea is not only that my words should please God, but also that the meditation of my heart, unheard by anyone else, would bring him pleasure too.

Now that's a slightly more scary thought because I can control my words much better than I can control my thoughts. Controlling what goes on in our wandering minds and wayward hearts is a much greater challenge. But it's a vital task. Psalm 51 says: 'Yet you desired faithfulness even in the womb; you taught me wisdom in that secret place' (verse 6). And, 'Create in me a pure heart, O God, and renew a steadfast spirit within me' (verse 10). Notice the emphasis on the inner world. God delights in 'truth' in our inward beings (see verse 6 ESV), the secret place in our hearts. That is, he loves it when we are sober in our judgement of ourselves, and are honest about who we are. However, 'truth' here doesn't just mean truth as opposed to falsehood. The Hebrew word is also used to mean faithfulness, dependability or stability, as when it is used of God, who is full of steadfast love and *faithfulness* towards his people (Exodus 34).

So David acknowledges in Psalm 51 that what God requires is inner truthfulness and stability of character, which he himself has failed to exhibit in the context of that psalm. Because, if you remember the background, he's just made a complete hash of his public *and* private worlds by getting someone else's wife pregnant, and trying to cover it up. When 2 Samuel 11 narrates that story, it concludes by saying: 'the thing that David had done displeased the LORD' (2 Samuel 11:27 ESV). So David confesses that what God delights in is truth in the inward being – even if we can get away with less in public for a while.

That emphasis continues in the psalm. David is taught wisdom in the secret heart. And then he prays in verse 10 for a clean heart and a renewed spirit. That is, he knows he needs more than public rehabilitation. He needs to be washed and made new *within* before he can please God.

Isn't it awesome to think that where David failed, where all of us fail, to please God – in the core of our being – Jesus did not? He always brought delight to his Father. Even his inner musings made his Father smile, whereas much that goes on in my head I am sure makes him frown, or worse.

Ephesians 4 talks about not grieving the Holy Spirit, who is God: 'do not grieve the Holy Spirit of God, with whom you were sealed for the day of redemption' (Ephesians 4:30). This is linked in the context with our words: 'Do not let any unwholesome talk come out of your mouths, but only what is helpful for building others up according to their needs, that it may benefit those who listen' (verse 29). But it is also connected to the inner turmoil of our hearts: 'Get rid of all bitterness, rage and anger, brawling and slander, along with every form of malice' (verse 31). As John Calvin comments on this:

> No language can adequately express this solemn truth, that the Holy Spirit rejoices and is glad on our account, when we are obedient to him in all things, and neither think nor speak anything, but what is pure and holy; and, on the other hand, is grieved, when we admit anything into our minds that is unworthy of our calling. Now, let any man reflect what

shocking wickedness there must be in grieving the Holy Spirit to such a degree as to compel him to withdraw from us.[6]

In your family

One aspect of our private lives which the Bible particularly addresses is our family life. How do we please God there? There are two places in Scripture where a family relationship is singled out and said to please God. The first is in Colossians 3:20, which says, 'Children, obey your parents in everything, for this pleases the Lord.' In Ephesians 6:1 the same command is given to Christian children, but it is said children should obey 'for this is right', rather than because it pleases God specifically. Both are true of course: what pleases God *is* what is right. In Ephesians 6:2, the apostle Paul backs this up by quoting from the Ten Commandments, 'Honor your father and mother'. Because the Old Testament law can still teach Christians a great deal about what is right and what pleases God, even though many of the things in the Old Testament have now become obsolete. As the Church of England's Thirty-nine Articles put it:

> Although the law given by God through Moses is not binding on Christians as far as its forms of worship and ritual are concerned and the civil regulations are not binding on any nation state, nevertheless no Christian is free to disobey those commandments which may be classified as moral.[7]

So the food laws and regulations about Temple worship are no longer applicable, and we don't have to run a modern society using civil laws from ancient Israel. But there are many moral laws in the

---

6 John Calvin, *Commentaries on the Epistles of Paul to the Galatians and Ephesians*, tr. William Pringle (Grand Rapids, MI: Baker, 1993), 1:301.

7 Article 7, in the updated English translation found in *An English Prayer Book* (Oxford: Oxford University Press, 1994).

Old Testament which remain valid, because they show us God's likes and dislikes, so we are not free to ignore them.

The New Testament also talks about pleasing God in our family lives in 1 Timothy 5:3–8:

> Give proper recognition to those widows who are really in need. But if a widow has children or grandchildren, these should learn first of all to put their religion into practice by caring for their own family and so repaying their parents and grandparents, for this is pleasing to God … Anyone who does not provide for their relatives, and especially for their own household, has denied the faith and is worse than an unbeliever.

So, Paul is giving Pastor Timothy some guidance on how to organise help for poor widows in his congregation. But before he gets into too many details, he puts the primary onus for their pastoral care fairly and squarely on their family. And did you notice what it is there that pleases God in particular? Showing godliness to one's own household and making some return to one's parents.

Now this is wider than just the idea of children obeying their parents. When people get married they leave their father and mother to form a new family unit with their spouses, and perhaps children of their own. But Paul still expects them to honour and look after their parents. This obligation even extends as far as our children, who are expected to have a concern for their grandparents too. And all this is part of family godliness. It's only one part of course – but it's a key part – and something we can forget in this age of state benefits. Verse 8 is especially sobering – to neglect our families is to displease God as much as rejecting the faith!

In your bedroom

There's one final area of our private lives which God is concerned with, and that's our sex lives. This can be a bit uncomfortable and embarrassing. But the Bible is so clear about this that we need to consider what it says very carefully. Let's look at what Paul writes in the earliest letter we have from him, 1 Thessalonians:

> As for other matters, brothers and sisters, we instructed you how to live in order to please God, as in fact you are living. Now we ask you and urge you in the Lord Jesus to do this more and more. For you know what instructions we gave you by the authority of the Lord Jesus.
>
> It is God's will that you should be sanctified: that you should avoid sexual immorality; that each of you should learn to control your own body in a way that is holy and honorable, not in passionate lust like the pagans, who do not know God; and that in this matter no one should wrong or take advantage of a brother or sister. The Lord will punish all those who commit such sins, as we told you and warned you before. For God did not call us to be impure, but to live a holy life. Therefore, anyone who rejects this instruction does not reject a human being but God, the very God who gives you his Holy Spirit.
> (1 Thessalonians 4:1–8)

It's noteworthy here that in verse 1, Paul refers to the basic initial instruction he gave to the young Thessalonian Christians before he was whisked away from them. And how does he refer to it? He taught them 'how to live in order to please God, as in fact you are living'. So teaching about living to please God is not a new idea at all, but something Paul must have done in Thessalonica for all new believers!

Sanctification, as Paul calls it in verse 3, or holiness of life, is God's will for us. As Richard Baxter rightly says:

> Holiness is pleasing to God himself; and therefore it must needs be pleasant to the saints that have it. For it is their end

and chiefest pleasure to please God. They know that this is the end for which they were created, redeemed, and renewed; and therefore that is the most pleasant life to them, in which they find that God is best pleased.[8]

The most pleasant life for us is a life that is pleasing to God first of all. This is why we were created, to be enjoyed by him. And as the famous Bible commentator Matthew Henry (1662–1714) was fond of saying, 'Whatever pleases God should please us.'[9] And what does pleasing God involve, according to 1 Thessalonians 4? Instructions given through the Lord Jesus – that is, at the very least, with the authority of Christ himself. Instructions about how to live holy lives. And specifically, in a sex-crazed society: teaching on sex. The word translated 'sexual immorality' covers a multitude of sins. It refers to any kind of sexual *activity* outside of heterosexual marriage, including incest, bestiality, homosexual practice, prostitution and heterosexual sex outside marriage. All of these things are displeasing to God. Just as much as cheating, lying, social and economic injustice and not caring for one's parents. And that's something every new Christian in Thessalonica was taught right from the start of their Christian lives.

Every kind of sex was on offer in Thessalonica, and it was considered perfectly normal to be having sex from a young age with different partners, whether male or female or both, whether you were married to them or not. So when preachers in the early church gave basic teaching about how to live a life that is pleasing to God, it had to include something about sex. It wasn't a secondary issue. It was something everyone needed to be taught as soon as they

---

8 Richard Baxter, *The Practical Works of the Rev. Richard Baxter*, ed. W. Orme (London: James Duncan, 1830), 10:339.

9 Matthew Henry, *Matthew Henry's Commentary on the Whole Bible: Complete and Unabridged* (Peabody, MA: Hendrickson, 1994), p. 1529 (on Jonah 4:1–4). See also p. 989 on Proverbs 16:3 and p. 1167 on Isaiah 46:5–13.

became Christians. If we want to please God and be holy, sexual purity is absolutely crucial.

Paul claims in 1 Thessalonians 4:8 that what he says comes with the authority of God himself. *He* didn't make it up. Such teaching can be found in the Old Testament, in places like Leviticus where that word 'detestable' – the opposite of what pleases God – is used of sexual sins (Leviticus 18:22, 20:13). It can also be found in other places. In 1 Corinthians 10 Paul goes through a catalogue of Old Testament incidents in which people were said not to please God. They include grumbling, revelry and idolatry, but also incidents of sexual immorality. And Ecclesiastes 7:26 warns against the seductive charms of an immoral woman:

> I find more bitter than death
> the woman who is a snare,
> whose heart is a trap
> and whose hands are chains.
> The man who pleases God will escape her,
> but the sinner she will ensnare.

So whatever we say about sex, let's be honest: it *is* important to God. Our private lives are God's intimate concern, and please or displease him as much as our public face.

This is precisely where a clash comes between what the Bible says and what our society says. Richard Layard encourages us to aim for whatever makes us happy. But what if the things that supposedly make *us* happy make *God* sad? That's certainly the case with illicit sex. Our society seems hell-bent on legitimising every form of sexual pursuit: if it makes *you* and the person you're doing it with happy, then go for it. But indulging our sexual appetites won't please us in the long run. The escalating cost in terms of disease, depression and divorce – the inevitable result of letting lust control social policy – should surely give pause for thought. But how much more should we pause when we hear that such passion-driven policies are displeasing to our Maker and Judge? Not just in the private sphere, but in the public square of our national life as well. Sometimes, as Jesus said, 'What people value highly is detestable in God's sight' (Luke 16:15).

God will have a lot to say to a culture which cracks down on smoking, while greed and lust and the suppression of truth are legalised and liberalised and left to fester. As the eloquent Victorian bishop J. C. Ryle (1816–1900) commented, 'Those who fear God more than man, and care for pleasing God more than man, are the best rulers of a nation, and in the long run of years are always most respected.'[10] He added:

> That which is morally wrong can never be politically right. To govern only for the sake of pleasing and benefiting the majority, without any reference to the eternal principles of justice, right, and mercy, may be expedient, and please man; but it does not please God.[11]

Do not aim at happiness

So should we aim at happiness, as a society? Do we have an unalienable right to it, as some think? Philosophers from Aristotle onwards have told us to 'seek happiness' above all, but that is not, paradoxically, the way to find it. The best way to *true* happiness is to seek to please God. As John Owen memorably declared, 'They must please God in this world who would be blessed with him in another.'[12]

Our true and best happiness only comes as a by-product of that greater quest. When we seek happiness for its own sake, and on our

---

10 J. C. Ryle, *Expository Thoughts on John* (New York, NY: Robert Carter & Brothers, 1880), 3:268 (on John 19:1–16).

11 Ryle, *Expository Thoughts on John*, 2:300 (on John 11:47–57).

12 John Owen, *The Works of John Owen*, ed. W. H. Goold (Edinburgh: Johnstone & Hunter, 1854), 24:35.

own terms, it tends to fly away and prove elusive. We were made to enjoy God and be enjoyed by him. But as Owen wrote:

> He that thinks to please God and to come to the enjoyment of him without holiness makes him an unholy God, putting the highest indignity and dishonour imaginable upon him. God deliver poor sinners from this deceit! There is no remedy; you must leave your sins or your God.[13]

True happiness is holiness.

Yet we must not think of God as reluctant to make us happy, or as somehow less delightful than all the things this world offers us. As John Piper assures us: 'God is the kind of God who delights most deeply not in making demands but in meeting needs.'[14] He himself is the inexhaustible fountain of delights, an eternal source of happiness that can never dry up. So if we come to him, we will find everything we ever dreamed of, only better, because we will have found *him*. As Augustus Toplady sang in his hymn 'Happiness Found':

> Happiness, thou lovely name,
> Where's thy seat, O tell me, where?
> Learning, pleasure, wealth, and fame,
> All cry out, 'It is not here:'
> Not the wisdom of the wise
> Can inform me where it lies,
> Not the grandeur of the great
> Can the bliss, I seek, create.
>
> Object of my first desire,
> Jesus, crucify'd for me!

13 Owen, *Works*, 3:575–6.

14 John Piper, *The Pleasures of God* (Fearn, Ross-shire: Mentor, 2001), p. 210.

All to happiness aspire,
Only to be found in thee:
Thee to praise, and thee to know,
Constitute our bliss below;
Thee to see, and thee to love,
Constitute our bliss above.[15]

Prayer

Almighty God,
who alone can bring order
to the unruly wills and passions of sinful humanity:
give your people grace
so to love what you command
and to desire what you promise,
that, among the many changes of this world,
our hearts may surely there be fixed
where true joys are to be found;
through Jesus Christ our Lord.
Amen.[16]

Something to ponder

1 How can you make sure that all your public and business activities
  are pleasing to the Lord, in their fairness, kindness and equity?
2 Are all your private activities pleasing to the Lord in truth,
  honour and holiness?
3 How is what the Bible says on these things so different from
  the world around you?
4 Praise God for the gospel which alone offers us solid joys and
  lasting treasures.

---

15 Augustus Montague Toplady, *The Works of Augustus M. Toplady* (London; William
   Baynes & Son, 1825), 6:398.
16 The Church of England's Collect for the Third Sunday before Lent in *Common
   Worship* (London: Church House Publishing, 2000), p. 389.

7

A treasured gift

Remember this: Whoever sows sparingly will also reap sparingly, and whoever sows generously will also reap generously. Each of you should give what you have decided in your heart to give, not reluctantly or under compulsion, for God loves a cheerful giver. And God is able to bless you abundantly, so that in all things at all times, having all that you need, you will abound in every good work. As it is written:

'They have freely scattered their gifts to the poor;
  their righteousness endures forever.'

Now he who supplies seed to the sower and bread for food will also supply and increase your store of seed and will enlarge the harvest of your righteousness. You will be enriched in every way so that you can be generous on every occasion, and through us your generosity will result in thanksgiving to God.

(2 Corinthians 9:6–11)

This chapter is about giving. Specifically, giving money. But it is not a guilt trip about money. I won't be appealing to you emotionally to increase your regular giving to church. It is not going to be a rousing altar call for you to give more to charity. I'm not going to talk about how rich you might be compared with the vast majority of our fellow Christians throughout the world. I am not going to include pictures of starving millions in a country you are unlikely to visit. This chapter will not contain lots of practical tips on saving money so you can give more of it away. And I'm not going to cover technical details about standing orders, gift-aid schemes and the receiving of collection.

It's not hard to spot how giving is an aspect of pleasing God. In 2 Corinthians 9:7, Paul tells us: 'Each of you should give what you have decided in your heart to give, not reluctantly or under compulsion, for God loves a cheerful giver.' Paul is writing here to the church in the southern Greek city of Corinth about what he calls in 2 Corinthians 9:1 'this service to the Lord's people'. That is, he's organising a large collection for impoverished Christians back in Jerusalem: Jewish Christians. And he's asking members of the churches he's planted – that is, predominantly Gentile churches – to make a contribution.

There's an obvious theological point being made here about the unity of the Jewish Christians in Jerusalem and the Gentile Christians in Corinth. Paul's collection or service for the saints back in Israel will demonstrate for all to see that his gospel really has had an impact on the Gentiles, who have turned to the Messiah, Jesus. As he writes to the Corinthians about giving to this collection, Paul gives us a model fundraising letter.

Not all of what he says is of direct relevance to us today. We'd have to go elsewhere in the New Testament for direct teaching about paying those who work in churches and that sort of thing (such as Luke 10:7 or 1 Timothy 5:17–18), but Paul's letter contains some general principles which will apply to all Christian giving. And he gets to this more generally applicable teaching at the end of his section on giving. So we'll be particularly looking at 9:6–15.

God loves a cheerful giver

Let's just unpack this statement about what God loves. 'God loves a cheerful giver', says Paul. So this is a theological statement, as it tells us about God. Just like everything else we've been looking at in this book, it tells us something about what God likes, what makes him smile, what he approves of.

This statement in no way contradicts what we learned in the previous chapters. We've heard that God loves sinners – that is, he loves rebels, those who fall short of his perfect standards of right and wrong, those who are far away from him. He seeks them out, and rejoices when they come home. So when Paul says God loves a cheerful giver he's not saying that God only loves people who give. Not at all. God loves people who *don't* give of their money. He loves the most penny-pinching, tight-fisted, mean-spirited people you can think of. He cares for them, and wants them to repent, to turn around, to come back to him, and come home.

So that's not what we're talking about here. We're not talking about how to get into God's good books, as it were. This is not how to be saved and get to heaven, but God does love a cheerful giver. He approves, values, enjoys and is pleased by a cheerful giver. This is a statement which helps us understand how we can glorify God and be enjoyed by him. It's a question of discipleship.

Isn't that hilarious?

So what exactly is a cheerful giver? It's quite important that we understand that, if we want to be one. And I assume we do want to be one, since God approves so highly of cheerful giving. You may have heard talks on this passage before; I know I have. And one thing that is sometimes said by preachers is that the word there translated 'cheerful' is the Greek word *hilaros*. It's the word from which we get our English word 'hilarious'. So you may have heard it said that God loves a hilarious giver. Which gives the impression that God approves of a kind of happy-go-lucky approach to giving, a free-floating, unthinking attitude which just throws money away. Or the more sophisticated version of this is to say *hilaros* is the Greek word from which we get 'exhilarating'. So God loves exhilarating giving, that is, exciting, bracing, thrilling, radical financial management.

I don't think that is what the apostle Paul is saying. I don't think it can be right to argue that because an ancient Greek word used two millennia ago sounds a bit like an English word we use today it must be related in meaning. That's what linguistic experts call 'semantic anachronism'.[1] It's perfectly possible that two words in two different languages separated by 2,000 years *might* be related or even close in meaning, but it's more likely that over the course of the centuries the meanings have moved apart, or at least become more nuanced. So we can't just say because 'hilarious' comes from *hilaros* that God loves a hilarious giver.

So what does *hilaros* mean? I think our Bible translators have got it right. In Paul's day it meant cheerful, joyful even. With overtones of graciousness, benevolence, gladness. You can see how it might turn into 'hilarious' over time, but I don't think Paul's thought has much to do with us rolling around on the floor clutching our stomachs in laughter as we throw away our cash to all and sundry.

To see what he's really getting at, it helps to see how the word is used in this context. In 2 Corinthians 9:7 it's used by way of contrast. Look at what Paul says again: 'Each of you should give what you have decided in your heart to give, not reluctantly or under compulsion, for God loves a cheerful giver.' So cheerful giving is opposed to reluctance and compulsion. The word for 'reluctant' is used to describe sorrow, pain or grief. Paul is saying that when we write out those large cheques to charity or our church, we shouldn't afterwards feel a piercing regret. We shouldn't be grudging or bitter about it.

He's not saying our giving shouldn't be sacrificial, or even hurt a bit financially. He's saying our attitude of heart, once we have made

---

1 D. A. Carson, *Exegetical Fallacies*, 2nd edition (Grand Rapids, MI: Baker, 1996), pp. 33–5.

our gift, shouldn't be 'Oh dear, I wish I hadn't done that! I wish I could take a zero off the end of that number. Can I have that cheque back? I need to change a 9 into a 3. I'm not sure I really wanted to give that much.'

This is clearly related to the phrase 'not under compulsion', because we feel most resentful about giving money away when we feel we have no choice: when we feel it's an obligation, a demand, a tax if you like. Paul has gone out of his way to make it clear to the Corinthians that what he's asking for is not a tax. So at the start of chapter 8 he praises the Macedonians who gave so generously, 'entirely on their own' (2 Corinthians 8:3). Throughout these chapters Paul says things like, 'I am not commanding you' (2 Corinthians 8:8), or that he wants any donation to be 'a generous gift, not as one grudgingly given' (2 Corinthians 9:5).

So clearly there was no obligation to contribute; no obligatory 10% tithe that they had to give. That Old Testament law doesn't apply to us directly as Christians. We can give 10 or 15 or 20% if we want to. As we earn more, some of us probably wouldn't miss 30%, but there's no law to dictate how much it should be. It's up to us. Indeed, that's what the first part of 2 Corinthians 9:7 says: 'Each of you should give what you have decided in your heart to give'. Or more literally, 'each just as he has decided before in his heart'. It should be a personal decision, carefully thought through and planned beforehand. So it's not a decision made on the spur of the moment as the plate comes round, or at the point of a sword, or because someone else is watching.

If we want to please God, if we want him to enjoy us, we need to be cheerful givers. Which means not giving reluctantly or because we think we have to, but giving generously and happily because we want to, not because someone else says we must. And that fits in well with Paul's constant focus in this letter on God's grace. It comes over most strongly, I think, in 2 Corinthians 8:9. Paul wants to motivate us simply by reminding us of Jesus: 'For you know the grace of our Lord Jesus Christ, that though he was rich, yet for your sake he became poor, so that you through his poverty might become rich.'

So, what pleases God? God loves a cheerful giver. Someone who happily gives of their own free will to support the gospel, motivated by the generosity of Christ himself. It doesn't say God loves a big giver. In a very real sense he doesn't care about the numbers. What matters to God isn't the amount of the gift – whether we give £1,000, £5,000 or £100,000. God is delighted by the heart of the donor, not the size of the donation.

Doing it for God

Remember what Jesus taught about the widow's offering?

> As Jesus looked up, he saw the rich putting their gifts into the temple treasury. He also saw a poor widow put in two very small copper coins. 'Truly I tell you,' he said, 'this poor widow has put in more than all the others. All these people gave their gifts out of their wealth; but she out of her poverty put in all she had to live on.'
> (Luke 21:1–4)

Jesus had much to say about giving and other so-called religious duties, such as praying and fasting. As commentator Don Carson explains:

> In each of these three traditional acts of piety, genuine Christian living is characterized by a simple yet profound desire to please God, and not by the ostentation that is in reality more interested in generating the impression among our peers that we are pleasing God.[2]

---

2 D. A. Carson, *For the Love of God: A Daily Companion for Discovering the Riches of God's Word* (Wheaton, IL: Crossway, 1998), 1:25.

Who we do these things for is the important thing, and that is actually immensely liberating. With some religious practices, such as Bible reading and going to church, it is possible to feel that we have done enough, we have done our duty. But with others such as giving and praying, we may sometimes have a lingering sense of guilt that we have not done as much as we could. There are always more people who need our prayers and our money! Yet if we do these things to please God, rather than simply to satisfy others, we can rest content. It is far easier for a Christian to please him than to impress and please everybody else. As the Puritan Richard Baxter said:

> If you resolve to give all that you have to the poor, if you do it to please God, you may attain your end: but if you do it to please them, when you have pleased those few that you gave it to, perhaps twice as many will revile or curse you, because they had nothing ... If you seek first to please God and are satisfied therein, you have but one to please instead of multitudes.[3]

God also knows and cares about where our money comes from, of course. He detests ill-gotten gains which come from sharp or illegal practices and businesses of which he does not approve (see Deuteronomy 23:18 for example). You can't please God by earning that way and then giving it away.

All that being said, the evangelist Billy Graham is credited with saying that our chequebooks are theological documents that show us who and what we worship. There's definitely something in that (even though chequebooks are rapidly becoming a thing of the past in the age of banking apps), because how I spend my money does say a lot about where my priorities are. Anyone reading my

3 Richard Baxter, *The Practical Works of the Rev. Richard Baxter*, ed. W. Orme (London: James Duncan, 1830), 2:560, 574.

bank statement can quickly see what I value most. But God can read hearts as well as bank statements. He knows if we give out of a sense of compulsion or because we've always done it. He knows when the cheerfulness has gone and the legalism has crept back in. A cheerfully given £10 makes God smile. But a reluctantly given £10,000 means nothing. He weighs the affection of our hearts, not the amount of treasure we hand over. Gifts given to his cause which come from a heart of loving faith 'are a fragrant offering, an acceptable sacrifice, pleasing to God' (Philippians 4:18).

The fruit of cheerful giving

God loves a cheerful giver, but Paul is sensitive to the Corinthians coming back at him and saying, 'Actually, Paul, we just don't think we can afford it. We're not convinced this is a good investment.' So he also works hard to show them that it's definitely worth investing in gospel work. And he does that by showing them what the fruit of their giving will be. I think there are two particular fruits of cheerful giving mentioned in 2 Corinthians: personal enrichment and the partnership of thanksgiving.

Personal enrichment

In 2 Corinthians 9:6, Paul gives us the basic principle of personal enrichment. He says, 'Remember this: Whoever sows sparingly will also reap sparingly, and whoever sows generously will also reap generously.' He's saying that the more you sow, the more you reap – and what is true in agriculture is also true in gospel finance.

Now, we have to be careful here, obviously. I don't want to give the impression that there's a simple and effective way to get rich, and that's by giving as much money as possible to Lee Gatiss Ministries Incorporated. I know that method of fundraising goes down well with some TV evangelists. But that's clearly not the point here. There's no prosperity gospel in the New Testament, whereby we give to God or to certain church leaders, and God in return makes us millionaires. That might be a disappointment to some of us, but it's not the way God works. He is not a slot-machine God.

However, when he says God loves a cheerful giver, Paul does actually mean that God *blesses* a cheerful giver. For a start, that phrase which we've just looked at is alluding to Proverbs 22:9 which says, in the Greek version Paul is quoting, 'God blesses a man who's cheerful and a giver.'

So Paul has slightly changed it from 'God blesses' to 'God loves', but the concept is the same and the next few verses show this. So he says in 2 Corinthians 9:8, 'And God is able to bless you abundantly, so that in all things at all times, having all that you need, you will abound in every good work.' In other words, God is perfectly able to look after those who are cheerfully generous with their money. They won't go short because of their generosity to others.

In verse 10 Paul adds, 'Now he who supplies seed to the sower and bread for food will also supply and increase your store of seed and will enlarge the harvest of your righteousness.' He picks up the concept of righteousness from an Old Testament quotation in verse 9: 'They have freely scattered their gifts to the poor, their righteousness endures forever' (Psalm 112:9). What he's saying is becoming clear. Don't *worry* about being a cheerful giver – God can look after you – he can keep you supplied, so that you can keep on being a generous giver, involved financially in many good works. So on the basis that those who can be trusted with little can be trusted with much (Luke 16:10), God will bless a cheerful giver so that they'll continue to have enough, so they can continue to be generous.

Paul concludes in verse 11 by saying, 'You will be enriched in every way so that you can be generous on every occasion'. I don't think we can entirely eliminate a material sense there. It's not all spiritualised – we will be enriched *in every way*, he says. But it is vital to notice that in this sowing and reaping, the sowing of material gifts is not said to reap an equivalent *material* harvest. The harvest is one of righteousness in verse 10. In other words, there's a spiritual blessing involved here, a spiritual enrichment. Now that may be on several levels. It certainly does *me* good to give a few thousand pounds to gospel work every year. I'm not talking about a warm pious glow of smug self-righteous satisfaction. It reminds me that life is not about having a large bank account and a luxurious lifestyle. It reminds me that my priorities are focused not on this world but the next. Where my treasure is, there my heart will be also (Luke 12:34). As Thomas Manton urges us:

> The sooner you begin to please God, the sooner you have an evidence of your interest in his favour, more experience of his love, more hopes of living with him in heaven. Oh! these things are not slight things! When once you come to taste the comfort of them you will be sorry that you had begun no sooner.[4]

The enrichment, this harvest of righteousness, includes seeing my money at work in gospel projects. So if our giving is directed towards the gospel, we will see gospel growth. We'll see the kingdom of God growing both in the world and in ourselves. If we're giving to support God's work in the world, then God will be at work in the world, and in us. And his work is not to make us rich, necessarily, in this life, but to make us righteous and holy, and to spread the good news of Jesus. If the point was to make us rich in this world, why did Jesus teach us to pray not for wealth but for 'our daily bread' (Matthew 6:11), alluding to Proverbs 30:8, 'Give me neither poverty nor riches, but give me only my daily bread'? Why did he who himself had no place to lay his head (Matthew 8:20) tell us to follow him by denying ourselves and taking up a cross daily (Luke 9:23)? Indeed, Paul also teaches that:

---

4 Thomas Manton, *The Complete Works of Thomas Manton* (London: James Nisbet & Co., 1872), 9:408.

godliness with contentment is great gain. For we brought nothing into the world, and we can take nothing out of it. But if we have food and clothing, we will be content with that. Those who want to get rich fall into temptation and a trap and into many foolish and harmful desires that plunge people into ruin and destruction. For the love of money is a root of all kinds of evil. Some people, eager for money, have wandered from the faith and pierced themselves with many griefs.
(1 Timothy 6:6–10)

The Christian life is about contentment, and loving God 'for better, for worse, for richer, for poorer, in sickness and in health'. Loving God and living to please him is the way to true happiness in this life and the next; loving money is the way to ruin and destruction – a grief-stricken path away from God, not the goal of our lives.

However, I wonder whether the reason we don't believe in the kind of spiritual enrichment Paul speaks of in 2 Corinthians 9 is because we've never actually tried the kind of generous giving he's talking about? We're often reluctant to part with our cash because we can't measure the harvest of righteousness promised in return. Or maybe we don't trust God that there'll be one? Or we don't think righteousness is something worth investing in? But I think we can trust God with the rate of return: there is no sounder investment. Our fluctuating financial fortunes in this life cannot be compared to the divine dividends we can look forward to if we cheerfully commit everything to God.

So that's the first fruit of cheerful giving: personal enrichment. God will enrich us in every way in return for our generosity. He *may* enrich us with sufficient money so that we can continue to be generous with it. But he will *certainly* bless us with an increasing harvest of righteousness, spiritual enrichment, both in the here and now, and in the world to come. 'Whoever sows to please their flesh, from the flesh will reap destruction; whoever sows to please the Spirit, from the Spirit will reap eternal life' (Galatians 6:8). As the great preacher John Chrysostom preached in the early church, 'For we were not born for this end, that we should eat and drink and be clothed, but that we might please God, and attain unto the good things to come.'[5]

The partnership of thanksgiving

There's also another fruit for cheerful givers to enjoy, according to 2 Corinthians 9:11–14. Generous giving to a gospel cause will also lead to the partnership of thanksgiving: 'You will be enriched in every way so that you can be generous on every occasion, and through us your generosity will result in thanksgiving to God.'

Paul is very much aware that the Jewish Christians back in Jerusalem might find it hard to accept help from these predominantly Gentile churches. To do so would acknowledge that these Gentiles really were brothers and sisters in Christ. Some would find that tricky theologically. But this gift would persuade them that something new really had happened in Christ. That should be a cause for thanksgiving, alongside the obvious gratitude for the material aid. So Paul says, 'Because of the service by which you have proved yourselves, others will praise God for the obedience that accompanies your confession of the gospel of Christ'. When they get this aid in Jerusalem, they'll thank God for you, and for what you've done – because it's been motivated by your acceptance of the same gospel they believe. In verse 13 it literally says they will glorify God because of your submission … and also because of 'the generosity of your *partnership* with them'. It's that important word often translated 'partnership' or 'fellowship' – *koinonia*. Money expresses our fellowship and unity with other Christians in a real and direct way, and by giving to gospel work we're joining in a gospel partnership.

---

5 *Saint Chrysostom: Homilies on the Gospel of Saint Matthew*, ed. P. Schaff, tr. G. Prevost and M. B. Riddle (New York, NY: Christian Literature Company, 1888), 10:153.

We have partnership with the gospel workers we support with our money, so this is another fruit of cheerful giving. It produces thanksgiving to God in the recipients. Those who are supported and touched through gospel giving will glorify God and praise him for *our* generosity. Because they'll realise that we give because God is at work in our hearts, convincing us of the truth of the gospel.

Just think how that principle might work at your church. So think of Mr and Mrs Brown whose daughter Susie lives near the church. They pray for her every day, but she continues to resist the gospel and reject the faith of her parents. Think how delighted they'll be when Susie meets one of the Christian mums in your midweek Bible-study group. Imagine how happy they'll be when Susie meets up one to one with the women's minister to study the Bible, and comes along to a Christianity Explored course. Picture the joy on their faces when Susie visits them at Easter and tells her mum and dad she's become a Christian. Hear them praying that night as they go to bed, 'Thank you, heavenly Father, for those people at the church, who cheerfully funded the ministry there to bring the gospel to Susie.'

Or what about Mrs Fagbemi, whose husband Ben works in a nearby city. He's always tried to be polite about her faith, but he's slightly sneering about Christianity because he thinks it's 'nice for women and children, but not for me'. Think how interested she'll be when he comes home and mentions that a chap at work has invited him to a Thursday lunchtime talk at a church near the office. Imagine her excitement as he recounts an interesting conversation about the gospel he had with a staff member on his table for lunch. Picture her delight as he comes home one Thursday saying he's prayed a prayer in the back of a tract he'd been given. Hear her praying, with tears in her eyes, 'Thank you, heavenly Father, for my brothers and sisters at that church, who cheerfully support that Thursday lunchtime service, and brought my husband the gospel.'

Or what about Dr Ahmed who lives in a country where it's not considered culturally acceptable to be a Christian. Think how amazed he will be when he meets a missionary your church helps support, who has left everything in his home country to sensitively bring the good news of Jesus to people like him. Imagine his surprise when he finds himself drawn to Christ through the life and work of this honest and sincere follower of Jesus. Picture the glint in his eye and the new gladness on his face when he turns to Christ and is filled with the Spirit after several deep conversations with him. Hear him praying one night, with gratitude in his heart, 'Thank you, Lord Jesus, for your people, who sent me this man so I could hear about you.'

Now, I don't know about you, but those stories brought tears to *my* eyes! And I just made them up, although they are based on real people I know. It would be far too overwhelming to get all the real-life Mr and Mrs Browns and Mrs Fagbemis who have been affected by the gospel work at our churches to come and tell us how grateful they are. Not to mention the Susies and the Bens and the Dr Ahmeds who've become Christians and been built up in their faith. Cheerful giving to gospel work will result in thanksgiving to God, as we join in partnership with others.

So God loves a cheerful giver. He enjoys watching us fill out those standing-order forms after prayerfully reviewing our giving. He is pleased by a generous, joyful heart which is not too attached to its wallet. Cheerful giving is good for us too. It brings personal enrichment for us in every way, and leads to a flood of thankful prayers to God from our partners in the gospel.

Prayer

God of all grace,
everything in heaven and earth is yours,
both wealth and honour come from you.
By your Spirit, inspire within us
generous hearts and ungrudging kindness

so that in everything we do, and everything we give,
praise and thanksgiving will rebound to you,
in the name of Jesus Christ, your Son, our Lord,
who is alive and reigns with you
in the unity of the Holy Spirit,
one God, now and forever.
Amen.

Something to ponder

1 What does your bank account reveal about *your* heart?
2 Could you cheerfully give more away to causes which please God?
3 What effects can you discern in your spiritual life from sacrificial giving?
4 Praise God for Jesus, who though he was rich, yet for your sake became poor, so that you through his poverty might become rich.

***

Now may the God of peace, who through the blood of the eternal covenant brought back from the dead our Lord Jesus, that great Shepherd of the sheep, equip you with everything good for doing his will, and may he work in us what is pleasing to him, through Jesus Christ, to whom be glory for ever and ever. Amen.
(Hcbrews 13:20–1)

The testimony of the ages

I have collected here, in chronological order, some of the choicest words from those I have quoted within the book, along with a brief note about who these saints of the past actually were.

Irenaeus of Lyon (130–200)
Irenaeus was a Greek Christian from Smyrna (in modern Turkey). He is especially remembered for his work as a bishop in southern France and for his book Against Heresies, *which defended the faith against early gnostic heresies.*

The more we have loved him, the more glory shall we receive from him, when we are continually in the presence of the Father.

John Chrysostom (347–407)
John was the archbishop of Constantinople (modern-day Istanbul) and famed as a 'golden-mouthed' preacher (which is what his Greek nickname 'Chrysostom' means). He was fearless in his denunciation of secular and ecclesiastical leaders, and a prolific writer.

For we were not born for this end, that we should eat and drink and be clothed, but that we might please God, and attain unto the good things to come.

Let, therefore, the man who undertakes the strain of teaching never give heed to the good opinion of the outside world, nor be dejected in soul on account of such persons; but laboring at his sermons so that he may please God (for let this alone be his rule and determination, in discharging this best kind of workmanship, not acclamation, nor good opinions). If, indeed, he be praised by men, let him not repudiate their applause, and when his hearers do not offer this, let him not seek it, let him not be grieved. For a sufficient consolation in his labors, and one greater than all, is when he is able to be conscious of arranging and ordering his teaching with a view to pleasing God.

Augustine of Hippo (354–430)

Augustine was a north African Christian and the bishop of Hippo (now known as Annaba, in Algeria). Having lived a hedonistic lifestyle, once he converted to Christianity at the age of 31 he became one of the most important and influential theologians and philosophers of all time.

Say not then, 'Tomorrow I will turn, tomorrow I will please God; and all today's and yesterday's deeds shall be forgiven me' ... God has promised pardon to your conversion; He has not promised a tomorrow to your delay.

But who can conceive, not to say describe, what degrees of honor and glory shall be awarded to the various degrees of merit? Yet it cannot be doubted that there shall be degrees. And in that blessed city there shall be this great blessing, that no inferior shall envy any superior, as now the archangels are not envied by the angels, because no one will wish to be what he has not received, though bound in strictest concord with him who has received; as in the body the finger does not seek to be the eye, though both members are harmoniously included in the complete structure of the body. And thus, along with his gift, greater or less, each shall receive this further gift of contentment to desire no more than he has.

Boethius (480–524)

Boethius was a Roman senator and consul, and a renowned historian and philosopher, as well as one of the most important Christian scholars of his day. He was imprisoned, tortured and executed for denouncing official corruption.

The supreme God is to the highest degree filled with supreme and perfect goodness. But we have agreed that perfect good is true happiness; so that it follows that true happiness is to be found in the supreme God ... So that we have to agree that God is the essence of happiness.

Gregory the Great (540–604)

Gregory was the bishop of Rome from 590 to 604, and a prolific writer. He famously promoted a mission to the Anglo-Saxons in England after meeting two blond-haired boys whom he described as 'not Angles, but Angels if they become Christians'.

For indeed in the judgment of Almighty God it is not what is given, but by whom it is given, that is regarded.

Thomas Aquinas (1225–74)

Thomas was a Dominican friar and priest from Aquino in Italy, and one of the most influential philosophers and theologians in history, particularly famous for his Summa Theologiae *(summary of theology).*

Whatever is desirable in whatsoever beatitude, whether true or false, pre-exists wholly and in a more eminent degree in the divine beatitude. As to contemplative happiness, God possesses a continual and most certain contemplation of himself and of all things else; and as to that which is active, he has the governance of the whole universe. As to earthly happiness, which consists in delight, riches, power, dignity, and fame, according to Boethius, he possesses joy in himself and all things else for his *delight*; instead of *riches* he has that complete self-sufficiency, which is promised by riches; in place of *power*, he has omnipotence; for *dignities*, the government of all things; and in place of *fame*, he possesses the admiration of all creatures.

John Wycliffe (1330–84)
Wycliffe was an English philosopher, theologian and Reformer from Yorkshire who opposed the pope and the doctrine of transubstantiation, and promoted the translation of the Bible into English. He was posthumously exhumed and burned at the stake as a heretic, but was later considered 'the Morning Star of the Reformation'.

If you wish to please God, you ought [to] detest pride in your thinking, in your mind, and in your life … the more humble a man is, the swifter he is in God's service.

Martin Luther (1483–1546)
Luther was an Augustinian friar and priest from Germany who became the pivotal inspiration for the Protestant Reformation. He wrote many works of theology and commentaries on the Bible as well as translating the Scriptures into his mother tongue.

It is not man's business to determine what pleases God; it is the business of God alone.

When the heart is impure and unbelieving, works do not please God, no matter how magnificent they are.

You should always be more pleased with a penny and God's approval than with a whole city full of guldens [gold coins] and his abomination.

Because we try to please God and not men, we bring upon ourselves the envy of the devil and of hell itself. We bear the slanders and curses of the world, death, and every evil. Thus Paul says here: 'I do not try to please men so that they will praise my doctrine and call me an outstanding teacher. I want to please only God. Whoever tries to please God will have men as his bitter enemies.'

What is right, that is, what pleases God, should be more important than wealth, body, honor and friends, grace, and enjoyment; and in this case there is no respecting of persons, but only of God.

John Calvin (1509–64)
Calvin was a French scholar–pastor exiled because of his Protestant faith to Geneva, Switzerland. He published sermons and commentaries on most of the Bible, as well as one of the most influential works of theology ever written, The Institutes of the Christian Religion.

God accepts our service as a father accepts his child's attempt to please him; they are far from perfect and amount to nothing, yet the father is content because he loves his child.

No language can adequately express this solemn truth, that the Holy Spirit rejoices and is glad on our account, when we are obedient to him in all things, and neither think nor speak anything, but what is pure and holy; and, on the other hand, is grieved, when we admit anything into our minds that is unworthy of our calling. Now, let any man reflect what shocking wickedness there must be in grieving the Holy Spirit to such a degree as to compel him to withdraw from us.

The Thirty-nine Articles (1563)

These articles were and are the doctrinal, confessional basis of the Church of England, and many of its global offshoots, ever since the Reformation. They express what the King of England's Coronation Oath calls 'the true profession of the gospel ... the Protestant Reformed religion'.

10. Of Free-Will.

The condition of Man after the fall of Adam is such, that he cannot turn and prepare himself, by his own natural strength and good works, to faith, and calling upon God: Wherefore we have no power to do good works pleasant and acceptable to God, without the grace of God by Christ preventing us [going before us], that we may have a good will, and working with us, when we have that good will.

11. Of the Justification of Man.

We are accounted righteous before God, only for the merit of our Lord and Saviour Jesus Christ by Faith, and not for our own works or deservings. Wherefore, that we are justified by Faith only, is a most wholesome Doctrine, and very full of comfort, as more largely is expressed in the Homily of Justification.

12. Of Good Works.

Albeit that Good Works, which are the fruits of Faith, and follow after Justification, cannot put away our sins, and endure the severity of God's judgment; yet are they pleasing and acceptable to God in Christ, and do spring out necessarily of a true and lively Faith insomuch that by them a lively Faith may be as evidently known as a tree discerned by the fruit.

13. Of Works before Justification.

Works done before the grace of Christ, and the Inspiration of his Spirit, are not pleasant to God, forasmuch as they spring not of faith in Jesus Christ; neither do they make men meet to receive grace, or (as the School-authors say) deserve grace of congruity: yea rather, for that they are not done as God hath willed and commanded them to be done, we doubt not but they have the nature of sin.

Richard Baxter (1615–91)

Baxter was a Puritan minister both inside and outside the Church of England during a turbulent century. He made his name as pastor of the church in Kidderminster and was one of the most prolific of the Puritan divines.

[T]hat is formally no good work, which is not intended chiefly to please God ... Moreover, the misery of the unconverted doth further appear in this; that while men are unconverted, nothing that they do can truly please God. There are many works which, for the matter of them, are commanded, which such men may do, but yet there are so many defects, and so much of the venom of their corruption mixt in them, that God hath no delight in them, but doth abhor them.

No man's works please God out of Christ, both because they are unsound and bad in the spring and end, and because their faultiness is not pardoned. But in Christ, the persons and duties of the godly are pleasing to God, because they have his image, and are sincerely good, and because their former sins, and present imperfections are forgiven for the sake of Christ.

Holiness is pleasing to God himself; and therefore it must needs be pleasant to the saints that have it. For it is their end and chiefest pleasure to please God. They know that this is the end for which they were created, redeemed, and renewed; and therefore that is the most pleasant life to them, in which they find that God is best pleased.

If you resolve to give all that you have to the poor, if you do it to please God, you may attain your end: but if you do it to please them, when you have pleased those few that you gave it to, perhaps twice as many will revile or curse you, because they had nothing ... If you seek first to please God and are satisfied therein, you have but one to please instead of multitudes.

John Owen (1616–83)

Owen was a Puritan minister, both inside and outside the Church of England, who served as Oliver Cromwell's chaplain and vice-chancellor of Oxford University during the short-lived English republic. He is known as the genius of English Puritanism for his many works, including a 2-million-word commentary on Hebrews.

For what doth please God, God himself is the sole judge.

They must please God in this world who would be blessed with him in another.

It is the gladness of the heart of Christ, the joy of his soul, to take poor sinners into this relation with himself. He rejoiced in the thoughts of it from eternity, Prov. 8:31; and always expresses the greatest willingness to undergo the hard task required for that.

He that thinks to please God and to come to the enjoyment of him without holiness makes him an unholy God, putting the highest indignity and dishonour imaginable upon him. God deliver poor sinners from this deceit! There is no remedy; you must leave your sins or your God.

William Gurnall (1617–69)
Gurnall was a Puritan minister within the Church of England, most famous for his multi-volume exposition of the 'armour of God' passage in Ephesians 6.

A frown or an angry look from God, whom the Saint so dearly loves, must needs go near the heart.

The Canons of Dort (1618–19)
The Canons of Dort are statements of Christian doctrine agreed on by the international gathering of Reformed theologians known as the Synod of Dort. They are foundational for many Reformed denominations today.

God seriously and most truly shows in His Word what is pleasing to Him, namely that those called would come to Him.

Thomas Manton (1620–77)
Manton was a Puritan chaplain to Oliver Cromwell who served as the minister of Covent Garden in London. He was famed as a preacher and was influential, through his published sermons, on many evangelicals in later generations, including Toplady, Spurgeon and Ryle.

The main intent of the soul must be to please God, as his will must be the rule of your life; so his glory must be the end of your lives.

A renewed heart, that is unfeignedly set to please God in all things, is more than all the pomp of external duties.

Whosoever will live happily with the Lord in glory must have a care to please him in the present life.

Whoever will please God in all things, and will purge his own soul and his life from sin, must take the word of God for his rule and direction.

So foolish is that Christian who is earnest for comfort, but taketh no care how to be directed and enabled to please God.

The sooner you begin to please God, the sooner you have an evidence of your interest in his favour, more experience of his love, more hopes of living with him in heaven. Oh! these things are not slight things! When once you come to taste the comfort of them you will be sorry that you had begun no sooner.

Alas! what a mean spirit have they that drive no higher trade than providing for the flesh, or accommodating a life which must shortly expire! Like foolish birds who, with great art and contrivance, feather a nest, which within a little while they leave. But how divine and god-like are they who look to higher things, to please God, enjoy communion with him, and live with him for ever!

Thomas Watson (1620–86)
Watson was an English Puritan preacher in London and a prolific author.

The snow covers many a dunghill. A snowy white profession [of faith] covers many a foul heart! The sins of professors [those who profess faith] are more odious. Thistles are bad in a field – but worse in a garden. The sins of the wicked anger God – but the sins of professing Christians grieve him.

Blaise Pascal (1623–62)
Pascal was a famous French Roman Catholic philosopher, scientist and mathematician whose book of Pensées (thoughts) is an eloquent and influential best-seller defending Christianity.

We are not satisfied with the life we have in ourselves and our own being. We want to lead an imaginary life in the eyes of others, and so we try to make an impression. We strive constantly to embellish and preserve our imaginary being, and neglect the real one. And if we are calm or generous or loyal, we are anxious to have it known so that we can attach these virtues to our other existence.

The Westminster Confession and Catechisms (1647)
The Westminster Assembly of Divines was a gathering of Reformed theologians during the Civil War period in London, eventually tasked with producing catechisms (Q & A style teaching documents) and a confession of faith to replace the Church of England's Thirty-nine Articles. They remain foundational for many Presbyterians.

Westminster Larger Catechism (Question 1):
Man's chief and highest end is to glorify God, and fully to enjoy him forever.

Westminster Confession (Chapter 11.5):
God does continue to forgive the sins of those that are justified; and although they can never fall from the state of justification, yet they may, by their sins, fall under God's fatherly displeasure, and not have the light of his countenance restored unto them, until they humble

themselves, confess their sins, beg pardon, and renew their faith and repentance.

Matthew Henry (1662–1714)
A Nonconformist minister from Flintshire in Wales, Matthew Henry was the author of a large and popular commentary on the whole Bible.

Whatever pleases God should please us.

George Whitefield (1714–70)
Whitefield was a prolific Church of England evangelist during the eighteenth-century revivals.

My dear friends, what is there in our performances to recommend us unto God? Our persons are in an unjustified state by nature, we deserve to be damned ten thousand times over. And what must our performances be? We can do no good thing by nature. 'They that are in the flesh cannot please God' [Romans 8:8]. You may do many things materially good but you cannot do a thing formally and rightly good because nature cannot act above itself. It is impossible that a man who is unconverted can act for the glory of God. He cannot do anything in faith and 'whatsoever is not of faith is sin' [Romans 14:23].

Augustus Montague Toplady (1740–78)
Toplady was a Church of England minister, historian, theologian and hymn-writer during the eighteenth-century revivals.

If God hath not wrought living faith in your heart, you have never performed one truly good work in your whole life.

Happiness, thou lovely name,
Where's thy seat, O tell me where?
Learning, pleasure, wealth, and fame,
All cry out, 'It is not here:'
Not the wisdom of the wise
Can inform me where it lies;
Not the grandeur of the great
Can the bliss, I seek, create.

Object of my first desire,
Jesus, crucify'd for me;
All to happiness aspire,
Only to be found in thee.
Thee to praise, and thee to know,
Constitute our bliss below;
Thee to see, and thee to love,
Constitute our bliss above.

Charles Simeon (1759–1836)

Simeon was a Church of England minister in Cambridge, England, and an important leader of the evangelicals within the church, who wrote a 21-volume set of expository sermon outlines on the whole Bible called Horae Homileticae.

It is not an occasional act of zeal that will please God, but a steady conscientious, uniform discharge of our duty.

It is in vain to think that we can ever please God, if we be not honest and just in all our dealings.

When we speak of any thing being 'an abomination' or 'a delight' to God, we mean only, that he will act in reference to that thing as we should towards any thing which excited such feelings in our minds.

J. C. Ryle (1816–1900)

Ryle was an evangelical minister (and later, the first bishop of Liverpool) in the Church of England, famous for his many tracts and his expository commentary on the Gospels.

Those who fear God more than man, and care for pleasing God more than man, are the best rulers of a nation, and in the long run of years are always most respected.

That which is morally wrong can never be politically right. To govern only for the sake of pleasing and benefiting the majority, without any reference to the eternal principles of justice, right, and mercy, may be expedient, and please man; but it does not please God.

Charles Spurgeon (1834–92)

Spurgeon was a prolific Baptist preacher and evangelist as the minister of the Metropolitan Tabernacle, a large church in London.

It should be the aim of every one of us to please God.

The greatest joy of a Christian is to give joy to Christ.

We cannot spend our lives in seeking the smiles of men, for pleasing God is the one object we pursue.

The best cure for the cares of this life is to care much to please God. If we loved him better, we should love the world far less, and be less troubled about our portion in it.

It is a wonderful thing, certainly, that we poor creatures should, by any means, be able to give pleasure to the infinitely-happy God; yet so we do when we trust him.

'Without faith it is impossible to please God,' but it gives God a divine pleasure to see the first grain of mustard seed of faith in a poor, turning sinner's heart.

As the man is, such is his work. The stream is of the nature of the spring from which it flows. He who is a rebel, outlawed and proclaimed, cannot gratify his prince by any fashion of service; he must first submit himself to the law. All the actions of rebels are acts done in rebellion. We must first be reconciled to God, or it is a mockery to bring an offering to his altar.

Ay, let me say it joyfully, the saving works of Jesus are lovely in the Father's eyes. Whenever our Lord Jesus says to a sinner, 'I absolve you,' it pleases God; whenever the Saviour calls a wanderer to himself and draws him to holiness by the attractions of his love it pleases God ... It is the pleasure of God that sinners should find a complete Saviour in Jesus. The Father has no pleasure in the death of the wicked, but had rather that he should turn unto him and live, but there is joy in the heart of God himself over sinners that repent ... Prodigals leaving their riotous living are pressed to the Father's bosom and cause pleasure to the soul of the benign Deity. Oh, returning sinners, you have not to ask Christ to appease the Father, for the Father himself loves you, and your salvation gives him joy.

'Well, what could I do that would please God?' you say. First, I should think you could look for his lost children. That is sure to please him. Go tonight, and see whether you cannot find one of the erring whom you might bring back to the fold. Would you not please a mother, if she had lost her baby, and you set to work to find it? We want to please God. Seek the lost ones, and bring them in.

In pleasing God there is implied an avoiding of all things which would displease him. We cannot say we 'do always the things which please him' unless we earnestly renounce the follies which vex his Holy Spirit.

B. B. Warfield (1851–1921)
Warfield was an American Presbyterian theologian at Princeton Seminary in the USA.

The purpose of the incarnation is therefore primarily to please God the Father, and to perform His will.

R. C. Sproul (1939–2017)
Sproul was an American Presbyterian pastor and theologian and a prolific author.

Every Christian should have a passion to please God. We are to delight in honoring Him. It should be our greatest desire to please our Redeemer.

Nothing is more pleasing to God than our sincere sorrowing over sin and turning from it.